Hamlyn all-colour paperbacks

Christine Metcalf

Cats

illustrated by Peter Warner

Hamlyn · London
Sun Books · Melbourne

FOREWORD

Keeping a pet is always more interesting when the owner learns all there is to know about the object of his affection. This book is a comprehensive guide for cat owners which it is hoped will add to the pleasure of keeping a cat. It describes how to select a kitten, how to look after your pet, and, for those proud owners who would like to present their cats for showing, there is a guide to exhibition procedure. I should like to acknowledge the kindness of the Governing Council of the Cat Fancy in allowing me to draw upon and quote the standards and scales of points for the many different breeds which are described and illustrated in this book.

Many other aspects of the cat are covered in this guide. The cat has played a variety of parts in the history of man. It has been both worshipped and feared, and since prehistoric times it has figured in religion and legend; sometimes it has been valued for its usefulness and more often for its grace and beauty. All its rôles are described in this book. Today the cat has become less important as a symbol, though superstitions about cats are still widespread, but it is increasing in popularity as a pet with people throughout the world who appreciate the individual charms of the animal. Whether you keep a cat for its affectionate companionship or because you admire its lithe grace and independence, there will be something of interest for you in this book.

The book will appeal mainly to cat-lovers everywhere, but it is hoped that there is something in it to interest even those who have yet to be converted.

C.M.

Published by The Hamlyn Publishing Group Limited
London · New York · Sydney · Toronto
Hamlyn House, Feltham, Middlesex, England
In association with Sun Books Pty Ltd, Melbourne

Reprinted 1972

ISBN 0 600 00080 X
Phototypeset by BAS Printers Limited, Wallop, Hampshire
Colour separations by Schwitter Limited, Zurich
Printed in England by Sir Joseph Causton & Sons Limited

CONTENTS

THE ATTRACTION OF CATS

People either like cats a great deal, or not at all. There seems to be no middle way. Cats possess a beauty all their own, a supple, silent strength that is not shared by other animals. They have the gift of direction. When separated from those they love they are often able to overcome enormous obstacles and cover great distances to be reunited with them. Yet at the same time they remain detached and aloof. For many, these are the characteristics that are their attraction. Dogs are animals that make noisy demands and display their affection, while cats are content to live alongside their owners, remaining remote, independent and inscrutable. The bland stare of a cat gives away nothing of its thoughts.

The cat family

When your cat is curled comfortably before the fire, or sitting on your lap contentedly purring, it is hard to associate it with the larger cats, the Cheetah, Leopard, Lion, Tiger, and others. But they are all members of one big family which scientists call Felidae. Generally the term *cat* refers to the smaller members of the genus *Felis*, but both small and large cats are closely similar in structure. All have five toes on the forefeet and four on the hind-feet. They bear sharp claws which can be retracted into sheaths. The only exception is the Cheetah which, although it has fully retractile claws, lacks the folds of skin which hide them when retracted. The teeth of all cats are developed to give a firm hold on struggling prey. They are sharpened into scissor-like blades which can pare meat from a bone.

The appearance of the Lion differs a little from other cats. It has long hair on its head and shoulders, called the mane. A tuft of hair also grows at the end of the tail. Female Lions do not have these distinguishing features and look more like other cats. Though the Lion is the most powerful member of the cat family it can be quite easily frightened.

The domestic cat and the Lion are both members of the family Felidae.

Domesticated cats

Biological science recognizes the name first given to a species. Carolus Linnaeus, the Swedish naturalist, called the domestic cat *Felis catus* in 1758. A later, often-used name is *Felis domesticus*.

Many theories exist concerning the origin of the domestic cat. The most commonly held view is that the earliest ones came from Egypt. It is generally accepted that the Kaffir (Caffre) Cat is the forefather of the European short-haired varieties, although there is no proof. The Kaffir Cat occurs in Syria and throughout Africa, including Egypt. It is smaller than the European Wild Cat, and is about the size of a large domestic cat. Its coat is short, and coloured yellowish buff toning to grey. Faint black marks occur on the body, the legs are marked by horizontal bands, and the long tail is ringed and tipped with black. It will breed freely with the domestic cat and can easily be tamed.

The Kaffir Cat

Varieties of cats

In the same way that Man is one species and one genus, with variants known as 'races', so all domestic cats throughout the world are of one genus and one species. For convenience, the variants are called breeds or varieties. They can be divided into three distinct categories: the *long-hair*, the *British short-hair*, and the *foreign short-hair*. Each group has specified standards to which it must conform for show purposes.

Many regard the long-haired cat as the aristocrat of the cat world. Regular brushing is necessary if the cat is to retain its full-coated glory. For many years it was thought to have developed from Pallas' Cat, *Felis manul*, but recent investigations have shown this to be unlikely. Pallas' Cat has a bushy tail and a long coat over a thick undercoat like the domestic cat, but the body and face markings are quite different.

The skull of Pallas' Cat (*below*) is broad, the narrow nasal bones broadening suddenly forwards, giving the face a shape quite different from that of other cats. The ears are set low, and the eyes high, on the head to enable the cat to peer over rocks without revealing itself.

Cats as hunters

The scientific definition of the domestic cat is 'a predatory mammal of the family Felidae'. It is a typical carnivore, with jaws and teeth adapted for eating flesh. In towns, the stray cats and, in the country, the feral cats hunt rodents, insects, and birds for food. Cats by their nature are hunters and it is wrong to suppose that a well-fed cat will not catch mice. On the other hand, many cats never become expert at rat destruction, because mice and rabbits are easier to catch. The cat relies on stealth and surprise to stalk its prey and, in suburban gardens, it earns the dislike of bird-lovers when it kills small birds. In fact, the percentage of birds killed and eaten is very much lower than that of rodents and insects. Without cats, vermin would soon increase to an alarming degree.

There have been many proverbs relating to cats and they occur in various forms and in many languages throughout the world. Two sayings concerning their hunting instincts are as follows: 'A cat is a lion in a jungle of small bushes,' and

'One needs to watch the cat at work to see the tiger in the hearth'.

Show cats and mongrel cats

Most household pets conform to no particular standards. They are mongrels, the result of free mating for many years. The show cage and the long pedigree are not for them, but nevertheless they are adored as much as any prize cat by their owners. Mongrel cats are more representative of the cat population than any described by the Cat Fancy organizations throughout the world. In Britain, the estimated cat population is around twelve million, and the United States now has approximately twenty-two million. Most of these cats are short-haired and may be any of the recognized colours, or variations of them.

The working cats of factories, farms and warehouses belong to the mongrel class. In fact it would be impossible for them to be otherwise. Unless a cat is kept under very close supervision, it will roam around and lose no time in finding a mate – cats are notoriously promiscuous.

HISTORY AND DISTRIBUTION

The earliest cats

In tracing the history and origin of the domestic cat, it must be considered together with all members of the family Felidae. Due to its wide distribution, the domestic cat is the best known member of the family of cats, large and small. Legends and stories of the cat date as far back as three thousand years before Christ, but there is evidence of its existence long before then. The most widely held view is that the cat was first domesticated by the Ancient Egyptians. Cats must have been known in India at about the same time, because occasional references are made in Sanskrit writings. It is not known when the first tame cat came to Europe, but the Phoenicians are credited with carrying Egyptian cats on their ships to foreign ports. Tame cats were possibly introduced into Britain when the Phoenicians visited the tin mines in Cornwall though many authorities believe that the cat did not reach Britain until Roman times.

The first approach in the long association between Man and the cat was probably made by the cat. From the earliest times, Man has been a gregarious being. The warmth and comfort of his camp fire would have attracted the cat. In these camps, food was easy to obtain, a factor which would have encouraged the cat to stay. In return, the value of the cat would have been appreciated by Man, when it reduced the number of rodent scavengers.

Going back even further, it is possible to link the cat with the extinct Sabre-toothed Tiger of prehistoric times. A skull of a Sabre-toothed Tiger of the Pleistocene Period, which began one and a half million years ago, was found in a cave in Brazil. It is similar to the cat in its skeletal and teeth formation. Other remains of the same era have been found in India, many parts of North and South America, Iran, Europe, and in Kent's Cavern and the Cresswell bone caves in the British Isles. Cats lived on the earth many millions of years before Man. Fossil remains from the Pliocene, Miocene, and even the Eocene Periods give evidence of their long existence.

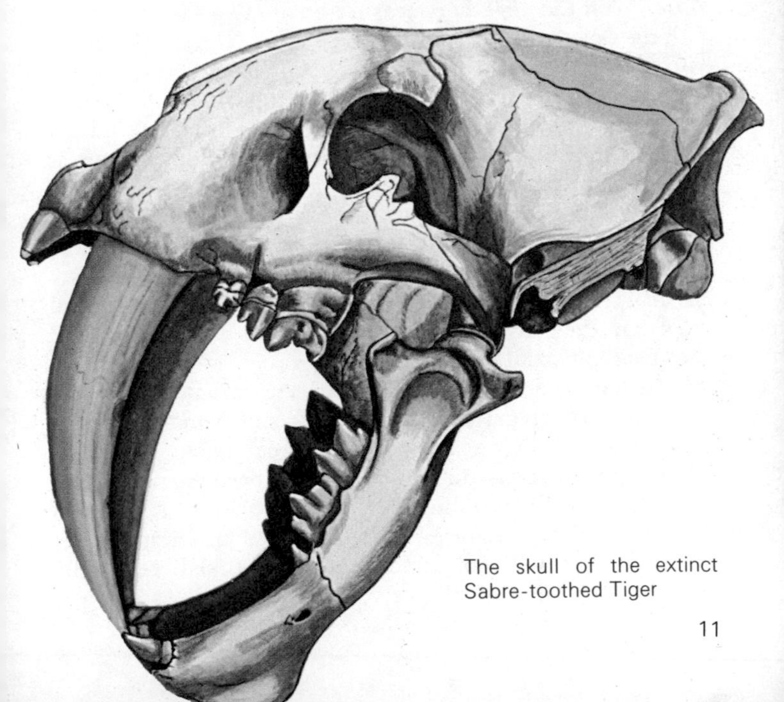

The skull of the extinct Sabre-toothed Tiger

Wild cats

Although the domestic cat in Britain resembles the Wild Cat, it is not a tamed descendent of the European Wild Cat. Had it been so, it would have been less highly regarded. In Roman times, the domestic cat was rare and valuable, whereas the Wild Cat was common in Britain until the early nineteenth century. In 1127, abbesses and nuns were forbidden to use furs more costly than those of rabbits or cats, and the cat was hunted in royal forests. Following the introduction of fire-arms and the destruction of the forests, the Wild Cat became almost extinct by the early twentieth century. In recent years, however, their numbers have been steadily increasing.

The European Wild Cat (*Felis sylvestris*) resembles the domesticated tabby, but the Wild Cat is more heavily built. It is reasonably easy to distinguish one dead specimen from another because the European Wild Cat has a larger skull and teeth than a domestic cat run wild, but difficulties occur when the two species interbreed. The head and body of the Wild Cat together measure about two feet in length, with the tail adding another twelve inches. The tail is marked with black rings and has a black tip. It ends bluntly and is uniformly thick from the top to the tip, whereas the tail of the domestic cat tapers to a point. The head of the Wild Cat is broad and square with abundant whiskers. The fur is thicker than that of the domestic tabby, yellowish grey in colour with black bands over the flanks and a black stripe running along the back. The Wild Cat leads a solitary life, and the male and female only come together for mating. The main diet consists of small mammals such as mice and voles but they also eat insects and hunt birds sometimes even tackling small deer or lambs.

In Britain, the Scottish Wild Cat (*Felis sylvestris grampia*) is the only survivor. It lives in rocky and wooded areas in the Highlands where it finds a safe retreat among the rocks. Following the increase in numbers, it has been moving southwards but is still confined to the Highlands. Reports of Wild Cats elsewhere are in fact feral domesticated cats. Although they will not attack unless provoked, both wild and feral cats will fight fiercely when cornered.

Comparison between the domestic cat (*below*) and the wild cat (*right*), showing the shorter thicker tail, stouter head and stronger build of the latter.

Early domestic cats

It has been discovered from frescoes and tomb paintings that the Ancient Egyptians possessed domestic cats. It is also known that the cat in India was domesticated at about the same time. Indian women are known to have used them to protect their stores of grain. The Indian Desert Cat, even now, is easily tamed when it is taken as a kitten and it is likely that this yellow, spotted cat with the brown ear tufts is an ancestor of the present-day spotted domestic cat found in India.

Great value was placed on domestic cats in early times. The Egyptians prized their cats so highly that it was strictly forbidden to export one. For this reason, a lucrative smuggling business was carried on by Phoenician traders and as a result, the domestic cat became known throughout the Eastern world and later found its way to Europe. The cat was known in China in 1000 BC and it appeared a little later in Japan. For centuries, domestic cats in both countries have been of service to the silk worm industry, protecting the cocoons from attack by rats.

The writings of the Greek historian Herodotus relate that the penalty in ancient Egypt for killing a cat was death. A Roman soldier who killed a cat was lynched by an enraged Egyptian mob. The household cat was prized by the entire Egyptian family. When a fire occurred the cat would be saved before attempting to put out the fire and when a cat died, members of the household were required by law to shave their eyebrows as a sign of mourning. The Ancient Egyptians used cats to catch birds for food.

Cats in early Britain were also held in high esteem. Hywel Dda, a prince of South Wales, passed laws in the ninth century on the worth of cats and their *tiethi* (qualities). He set the value of a kitten from birth until its eyes were open at one penny. From that time until it could kill mice, it was valued at two pence. The penalty for killing a cat was fixed at its worth, measured in corn.

We have gained our opinion of the value of cats from the many stories and legends that have been handed down to us. More stories about cats are on record than about any other animal. One story tells us that when Noah had completed his ark and had taken into it a pair of all the animals of the world, there were no cats, because at that time cats did not exist. The rats and mice bred so rapidly that soon the ark was overrun and food became a major problem. In desperation, Noah asked the Lion if he could help in any way, because the Lion was king of all beasts. The Lion sneezed and, from his nostrils, two cats, miniatures of himself, came forth. The cats immediately set about the vermin population, greatly reducing their numbers. The surviving rats and mice were so frightened that they hid in holes and they have lived in this way ever since.

Invading Roman armies possibly brought the domestic cat to Britain.

The Chinese have a legend which tells us that the cat is the result of a cross between a lioness and a monkey. The lioness gave to her progeny dignity, and from the monkey came playfulness and curiosity, all characteristics of the domestic cat.

The Ancient Greeks seem to have had little interest in cats. A drawing of a cat appears on only one ancient Greek vase. On the vase, the cat is being led by a slave. No records exist indicating that cats were adopted as household pets. The Romans, on the other hand, made much of the cat. The invading Roman armies must certainly have taken cats with them. The remains of a cat found in a Roman villa at Lullingstone in the British county of Kent is evidence of this. St George Mivart, an authority on cats, who wrote his book *The Cat* in 1881, believed that until the arrival of Julius Caesar there were no domestic cats in Britain. Of course, a large number of Wild Cats roamed the country.

The domestic cat did not become common in France until the middle of the thirteenth century. Until then, the genet, a member of the civet family, was used as a mouse killer.

Over the years, cats have continued to hold a special place in communities throughout the world. Many things have been taxed, including windows, births, deaths, marriages, dogs and even hats. But cats have never been taxed.

Where cats live

The earliest members of the cat family lived in Asia, Europe and North Africa and have spread from there over the world. The spread to Ethiopia and the Orient was not too difficult, but cats reached South America much later in time, because this was, for long periods, an island continent. No cats reached the Australasian region until they were taken by Man, for the area was too inaccessible.

Once these different regions were colonized the cats tended to diverge from their other isolated relatives, and form new species. Within the classification used today, however, cats are thought to all form a family, the Felidae, in which there are four genera and thirty-six species. It is easy to observe how the cat loves warmth, and almost all the members of the group Felidae dwell in the warmest regions of the earth. No region is too hot for certain species, but none dwell in the extreme north with the Polar Bear. The Snow Leopard, protected by an ample furry coat, is found on the snowy heights of Tibet and a group of lynxes are found in Scandinavia and Canada. But the greatest variety of cats live in warmer climes. Many of the wild cats will interbreed freely with local domestic cats.

The only surviving European native cat is *Felis sylvestris,* the European Wild Cat. This animal feeds mainly on small mammals and birds, but it has been extensively hunted and destroyed because it also sometimes attacks poultry and lambs. Today the numbers are greatly reduced and it is comparatively rare.

Two hundred years ago, the Wild Cat could still be found in parts of England and Wales and over wide areas on the European mainland. In Britain it now lives only in the Scottish Highlands, where, in the deer forests, it helps to keep down the hares that spoil the stalkers' approach. In plantations of young trees, the Wild Cat checks the spread of rabbits and other vermin which damage the shoots. In continental Europe, the chief stronghold of the Wild Cat is in the mountains of Eastern Europe, the Balkans and Asia Minor. Conditions in Ireland would seem to be suitable for the Wild Cat but, for some reason, it never seems to have existed on that island.

Felis sylvestris, the European Wild Cat

Cats around the world

The Lion, Leopard, Snow Leopard, Clouded Leopard, Cheetah and Caracal, and a variety of smaller cats, are all inhabitants of the Old World. Cats were absent in South America until the Panama land bridge connecting North and South America was re-established in the Pleistocene Period. The Puma, Jaguar, Ocelot, Jaguarondi and some other cats belong exclusively to the New World. The cats of the Old and New Worlds are quite distinct and lynxes are the only cats common to both.

Among the American cats, a division may be drawn between North and South America, only the Puma being common to both areas. It covers a wide range of climates, including plains, forests and deserts. Few animals have so many common names, and in the United States alone, the Puma is called the 'Cougar', 'Mountain Lion', 'Painter', and 'Catamount'.

Lynxes are found in many parts of the world. The range of the Northern Lynx includes all the temperate forests of the northern hemisphere. The Caracal Lynx to some extent

Below, from left to right: The Cheetah, the Ocelot, the Snow Leopard and the Caracal Lynx

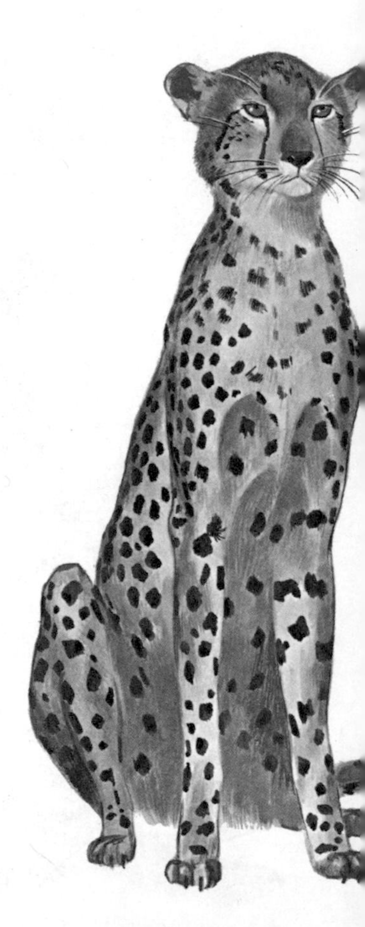

replaces the Northern Lynx in the warmer parts of the Old World. The Caracal is of medium size with a very short tail and its sharply pointed ears carry tufts of hair at the tips. The colour varies from pale sandy grey to rusty red, and its underparts are white. Lynxes are good swimmers, poor runners, but tireless walkers.

Asia is the great home of the cat family. No cats are native to the West Indies, nor to Madagascar, in spite of ideal conditions. Australia, New Zealand and the Oceanic islands are without a single indigenous cat of any kind.

CATS IN RELIGION AND FOLKLORE

Veneration of cats

The cat, more than any other animal, has played its part in legend and mythology. Through the ages it has been a symbol of good and evil, of religion and black magic, of light and darkness. The Ancient Egyptians worshipped and revered the cat and tomb paintings, frescoes and carvings are evidence of this. Some form of cat worship continued in Europe until the fifteenth century, when Pope Innocent VIII ordered the Inquisition to search out cat worshippers and have them burnt as witches.

At first, veneration for the cat probably arose from its usefulness to the national economy, because it protected stores of grain. Japanese stories tell how cats were kept in temples to protect sacred manuscripts. Confucius is said to

have had a favourite cat. The British Museum has many pictorial representations of the cat in Ancient Egypt, showing the honoured position which cats occupied in society under the pharaohs. One such picture is from an eighteenth dynasty tomb, dated 1684 BC. It depicts a wild-fowling scene, showing a cat eagerly waiting to leap from a boat to retrieve a bird from the reeds for its master. Many other wall paintings show the cat in domestic, as well as religious, situations.

Although many of the stories of cats in religion are

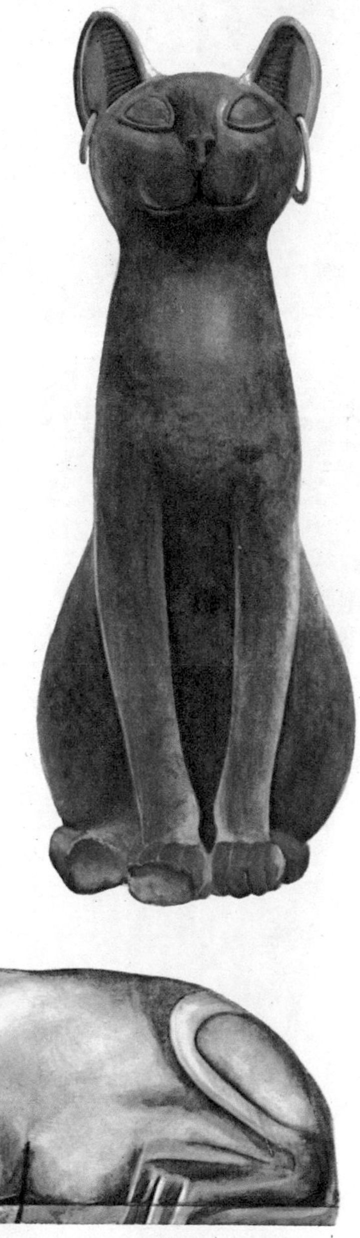

Figures and talismans of cats were made from all types of materials and can now be viewed in museums.

Muslim in origin, it is interesting to note that Hebrew writings did not refer to them. Only one reference to cats occurs in the Bible, and that is in the Book of the Apocrypha, Baruch VI v. 22. In this reference, Baruch is describing the gods of the Babylonians. He states: 'Upon their bodies and heads sit bats, swallows and birds, and the cats also.' The spread of Christianity reduced the importance of the cat as an object of worship.

Terror of the unknown has haunted the lives of primitive peoples through the ages. People believed that by means of ritual and incantations Man could command and control the deities. In order to obtain his supernatural power, Man identified himself with animals. Cats and serpents figured most often as totem animals.

Herodotus, who travelled in Egypt about 450 BC, described the shrine of the cat-headed goddess Bast as 'standing on an island completely surrounded by water, except at the entrance pas-

Many mummified bodies of cats have been found in Egypt, testifying to their ancient importance. With them were buried funeral offerings.

sage. It was built of finest red granite, the vestibule sixty feet high and ornamented with handsome figures six cubits in height.' Bast is often represented bearing a *sistrum*, a sacred musical instrument with a cat marked upon it as an emblem of the moon. Oldfield Howey tells us in his book *The Cat in the Mysteries of Religion and Magic* of a similar instrument, called a *samisen*, used by the singing girls of Japan. The strings were made of cat-gut. The geishas of Tokyo once subscribed for a funeral service for the souls of the cats whose lives had been ended to provide material for the instruments.

An extraordinary variety of cat mummies have been discovered in Egypt. Some are wrapped in linen bandages, forming a pattern of two colours. Linen discs were sewn on to represent eyes and nostrils, and midribs of palm leaves represent the ears. Others have been found in mummy cases of wood, bronze or clay.

From the Ancient Egyptian goddess Bast, or Pasht, may have originated the name 'puss'. Pilgrims came to her temple to celebrate the feast of Diana.

Cats in art

Despite the lack of references to the cat in the Bible, Christian art, and Christian painting in particular, has often featured the cat. Leonardo da Vinci was fond of producing studies of the Virgin and Child. In many of these works, he introduced a cat, or a cat with her kittens. The sixteenth-century Flemish painter, Frans Floris, painted a scene of the Garden of Eden, with a cat at the foot of the Tree of Life. An engraving by Albrecht Dürer in 1504 shows a cat sitting at this same tree with its tail curled about the legs of Eve.

According to an Italian legend, when Mary gave birth to Jesus, a mother cat gave birth to kittens at the same time, and in the same manger. Italian artists influenced by this story have often painted this scene and it is also said that a kitten, descended from those born in that manger, bears a cross-shaped marking on its back.

Louise Elizabeth Vigée-Lebrun (1755–1842) was famous for her portraits of Marie Antoinette and other members of the court of Louis XVI. She is also noted for her painting of a beautiful group of the Holy Family. In this the child Jesus is asleep and his mother is seen lowering him into his cradle, watched by his father and other members of the family.

Albrecht Dürer engraved a cat at the feet of Eve as she stood beneath the Tree of Life.

Cats have been associated with many of the saints, especially St Francis of Assisi, around whom animals were supposed to have flocked.

The homely scene is completed by the cat dozing beneath the stove in the corner.

Some other artists whose works have included cats are Bassano, Reynolds, Gainsborough and Renoir.

Cats have been associated with the saints of the early Church, including St Patrick. This association may have marked the beginning of the use of cats in church architecture during the early years of the Christian Church. The cat is also painted as companion to St Yves, patron saint of lawyers, and to St Francis of Assisi, who took to a life of poverty and founded the Franciscan order of monks.

Cats and symbolism

In northern Europe too the cat appeared in a religious setting. The ancient goddess of love and beauty was known as Freya. To her worshippers, she was the goddess of fruitful love and her chariot was drawn by a pair of cats. This was appropriate, considering the lithe beauty and fecundity of cats.

The husband of Freya was Odur, god of the summer sun, another connection with cats. The cat is a symbol of the sun in Egyptian mythology. The Ancient Egyptian sun-god, Ra, assumed the form of a cat in order to combat the power of evil. The most formidable of his serpent antagonists was Apap, who dwelt in the deepest gloom of the other world. In his cat form, Ra would battle daily with the powers of darkness and evil. The celestial cat would leap upon the reptile and Apap would return, torn and bleeding, to the other world.

Japanese mythology includes a story of a vampire cat. It is said that the Prince of Hizen, when leaving the garden at sunset with his favourite lady, O Toyo, was followed by a large cat. The lovers parted for the night, and the cat followed O Toyo to her bedroom. She was soon asleep but she awoke at midnight to see the cat poised to attack her. Before she could cry out, the animal strangled her. It buried her beneath the veranda and assumed her human form.

Ra, the Egyptian sun-god, combats the evil serpent.

The vampire cat of Japanese mythology

The Prince knew nothing of this but soon after the occurrence he fell ill. Doctors were unable to discover the nature of his complaint but as his condition worsened at night they set guards to keep watch. They always fell asleep just before the stroke of ten, until one loyal soldier, Ito Soda, contrived to keep awake by thrusting his dagger into his thigh. He saw the beautiful woman approach the Prince but his presence prevented her from casting her evil spell. Ito continued his watch and the Prince began to get stronger. Convinced that O Toyo was really a ghoul, Ito made plans to slay her. As he attempted to strike her with his dagger, she took the form of a cat and sprang away, escaping to the mountains where she was finally slain by hunters.

Cats and superstitions

After an early association with holiness, cats were later connected in popular belief with witchcraft. Witches were supposed to keep a cat as an animal familiar. People firmly believed that witches sometimes took cat shape themselves. Even as late as 1718, William Montgomery of Caithness, in Scotland, declared that hordes of cats gathered round his house, talking in human language. One night, he killed two and wounded several others with a hatchet. The next day, two old women were found dead in their beds, another had a bad cut on her leg, for which she would not give an explanation. He was convinced that they were the witches who assumed cat shape.

In Britain, the black cat is generally considered lucky. To meet a black cat is usually thought to be fortunate, especially if it runs across one's path. There are, however, some variations of this belief. In eastern Yorkshire, it is considered lucky to own a black cat but unlucky to meet one. Some people believe good fortune will only come to those who stroke the animal three times. Some say the omen is bad if the animal runs away, or crosses the path from left to right. To meet a white cat is an ill omen in any circumstances in Britain, but in the United States, Belgium, Spain, and some other European countries, a directly opposite belief prevails. In South America black cats are believed by some to be a powerful hoodoo, causing bad luck, disease and death.

In the county of Sussex in Britain, a kitten born when the blackberry season has just ended is called a *blackberry cat*. It is expected to be extremely mischievous. Kittens born in May are sometimes said to be unlucky. If a cat leaves a house when there is illness, and cannot be encouraged to return, the sick person is not expected to recover. If the household cat sneezes near the bride on her wedding morning, the marriage will be a happy one. If a cat sneezes three times, all the family will have colds before long. On the Yorkshire coast of Britain, wives of fishermen believe their men will return safely if a black cat is kept in the house.

A 'rat-scare' from a house in Southwark, England

Cats and literature

'A kitten is so flexible that she is almost double; the hind parts are equivalent to another kitten with which the fore-part plays. She does not discover that her tail belongs to her until you tread upon it.' So wrote the American philosopher Henry David Thoreau. Most cats are friendly, playful, yet at the same time detached. Perhaps this explains why cats are often referred to in literature. In the *Merchant of Venice,* Shakespeare describes the cat as 'the harmless necessary cat'; and in *Henry V,* he refers to 'playing the mouse in absence of the cat.'

Chaucer realized the contrariness of cats when he wrote:

Let take a cat, and foster him well with milk
And tender flesh, and make his couch of silk,
And let him see a mouse go by the wall,
Anon he waiveth milk, and flesh, and all,
And every dainty which is in that house,
Such appetite hath he to eat a mouse.

Many children's stories feature the cat. A well-loved friend of childhood is *Orlando, the Marmalade Cat* and Alice's Cheshire Cat is known to all. We would have been less familiar with Dick Whittington had his lengendary cat not been in the story. One of Rudyard Kipling's most famous stories is *The Cat that Walked by Himself*. A cat can make friends with anything, and this fact has formed a basis for many stories and rhymes, such as Edward Lear's nonsense poem 'The Owl and the Pussycat'. A modern adventure based on this same theme of friendship was *The Incredible Journey* by Sheila Burnford. After the beginning of the nineteenth century, when the witch hunting terror had ceased and the cat had once again found favour, several nursery rhymes about cats were written for children.

Every cat owner is aware of the individual personality of his cat, and this individuality can stimulate the imagination of the writer of children's stories.

Three popular animal characters; the Cheshire Cat from *Alice in Wonderland* and the Owl and the Pussycat from the poem of the same name.

Cats and the weather

Many rural superstitions connect the behaviour of cats with the weather. When the cat washes its face, some say that it is a sign of rain. If it washes its face in the parlour, then company can be expected. Welsh sailors believe that constant mewing by the ship's cat foretells a difficult journey. If the ship's cat is playful, sailors expect a strong wind astern. Someone wishing to upset the voyage can raise adverse winds by confining the ship's cat beneath a pot. It is said that a cat looking out of the window is looking for rain.

A cat's sneeze means rain. Indonesian and various Malay people believe that bathing a cat will bring rain. When cats run about wildly, clawing at curtains and cushions, it means that wind is coming. When they sit with their backs to the fire, look out for frost or a storm. To throw a cat overboard at sea raises an immediate storm. But because it is considered lucky to have a cat on board, no sailor would dream of treating a cat in this way. In fact, it is extremely rare to hear of a shipwreck where the cat was not among the first saved.

Cats were among the first saved at a shipwreck.

In the former province of Bohemia, in western Czechoslovakia, the cat is regarded as a symbol of fertility. One buried in a field of grain will guarantee a good harvest.

Never kick a cat or you will get rheumatism; never drown one or the devil will get you. Throughout the world it is considered bad luck to maltreat a cat. This world-wide respect for the cat is probably rooted in those ancient religions in which the cat was the sacred animal, and in which retribution would fall on anyone who harmed it.

A cat clawing at the curtains is supposed to indicate that wind is coming.

Cats in heraldry

Armorial or heraldic insignia have been in use for so long that authorities differ about their origin. Some authorities trace their source to Ancient India and China. Others suggest that the beginnings are to be found in the national banners and shields of Egypt and Mexico. The signs borne on a shield were used during the Crusades to distinguish knights in the field. They later appeared on personal apparel, books, seals, signet rings, windows, furniture and tapestry hangings. The cat is one of the creatures frequently portrayed in heraldry.

With the fall from grace of the symbolic cat, after the

Members of the cat family have been used in many different forms in heraldic coats-of-arms and emblems. The Lion appears on the standards of many royal houses as a symbol of courage and nobility.

Republic of France had taken it for use on its banner, the cat almost ceased to be the emblem of noble houses. It was used extensively, however, for tradesmen's signs. Domestic servants leaving their master took the family crest for their own use and we see the cat displayed by many ex-servants who turned to trade.

In ancient times, the name of every person or place had a symbolic meaning. Many crests were a pun on the name of the possessor. The old Scottish Clan of Chattan adopted the Mountain Cat for their crest. The English Catesby family adopted a Spotted Cat, which can be seen on a stained glass window in Lapworth Church in Warwickshire.

CHARACTERISTICS AND ANATOMY

Independence

Throughout long years of domestication, the cat has retained its independence. Whereas the dog has become entirely dependent on Man, the cat will hunt for food, find a warm place to sleep and keep itself clean. Cat lovers know that the belief that cats do not attach themselves to people but to places is a fallacy. Many reports exist of cats that have travelled great distances over unknown country to find their owners, indicating that cats have a quite remarkable homing power. The fact that cats survive long, arduous journeys and arrive at their destination fit and well demonstrates that they intelligently allow time for resting and feeding.

It is impossible to generalize about cats because they all behave differently. All have their likes and dislikes, but they all share one characteristic, which is that they prefer a solitary existence. Dogs let out on their own will seek the company of other dogs, because they are pack-minded. The cat likes 'to walk by itself'.

Language

Cats possess the power to express themselves by sounds and gestures to such a degree that the language of cats is a study in itself. All cats have their own way of communicating with their owner. When you acquire a new cat, you have to begin to understand and interpret its signs. Many of the signs are common to all cats. Everybody knows that a contented cat purrs. Cats miaow to humans, but not to other cats. A form of greeting common to most domestic cats is the *chirrup*. They also have an astonishing vocabulary of mews, growls, hisses, screams, spits, and caterwauls, for use on different occasions. A cat also uses facial and bodily expressions to make itself more readily understood. A cat's face can express pleasure, pain, contempt, and fright. Ears pointed forward express joy and expectancy, whereas when its ears are laid flat against the head, you know that your cat is angry.

Dignity

Most people believe that cats do not like water. It is true to say that many do not like even getting their feet wet. On rainy days, some domestic cats will wait indoors for hours for the weather to change. While most cats prefer to keep their fur dry, many of them do enjoy playing with water. They can be seen waiting for the drips from a tap, splashing water from a basin, or playing with a stream of water from a hose. Some cats may be descended from the fishing cats of the Orient. Many domestic cats will enter fresh or salt water to capture their prey and, on the west coast of Scotland, Wild Cats live almost completely on fish. At low tide, they can be seen clawing fish out of the water.

A cat will not endure loss of dignity. For this reason, you cannot teach it to do any trick that is not to its own advantage. Intelligence tests normally carried out with animals, such as mazes and coloured discs, are of little use when applied to cats. The animal has a mind of its own, is notoriously disobedient, and will not learn the most simple trick if there is nothing to be gained from it. On the other hand, the cat will perform a difficult feat in order to gain a desired objective. Do not expect instant obedience from the cat. It will make up its own mind.

Living with dogs

Dogs will often chase cats, but it is wrong to suppose that they are natural enemies. Cats and dogs will live happily together. Once they are settled jointly in a household, they will become the greatest friends. Nothing gives a more delightful picture of domestic bliss than to see them curled comfortably together before a fire on a winter evening. If you intend to keep both a cat and a dog, you should have them both as young animals and let them grow up together. Even when adult they will soon accept each other, as long as they are kept in separate rooms to begin with, until each becomes accustomed to the scent. Great care must be taken when a new kitten arrives in a house where an adult dog, who is not used to having a cat around, is already living. If the dog gets curious and alarms the kitten, it may harm the dog's eyes with its claws.

Walking and climbing

The similarity between the domestic cat and the wild members of the cat family does not stop at outward appearance. All cats have many common characteristics. They move in the same way, walking on their toes rather than the soles of their feet and the soft pads, on which the hunting cat can move so quietly, are also on the toes. Cats are able to move at great speed, covering the ground in huge leaps, but they do not run like the dog or most other animals. Cats move front and back legs on one side and then front and back legs on the other side, like the giraffe and the camel.

The Lion and the Tiger are both too heavy to be expert climbers, and the Cheetah, the fastest of all mammals, has no need to do so. But all other cats are expert climbers. The domestic cat often finds a favourite relaxing place in a tree or on top of a garden shed.

Reactions

Domestic cats retain many of the characteristics of their wild relatives. In the face of danger, the cat can be transformed to a snarling, hissing fury. Unlike the dog, which may run off, the cat will often stand its ground, with arched back, relying on its tremendous muscular energy and flexibility. By raising its back, the cat can make itself look bigger than it really is. The cat does not arch its back through fear, but as an intimidating gesture. Many a dog has come off worse in a fight. Most dogs will not stay to take the risk.

The cat is a naturally cautious animal. It will not rush foolishly into situations without first taking stock. At night, when it is let out, it will hesitate in the doorway while its eyes adjust to the changed light. Its response to sudden movement or noise is immediate.

In a fight, the arching of a cat's back is not a reaction of fear but an intimidating gesture designed to make it appear bigger than it is.

Eyesight

According to popular belief, cats can see in the dark. But cats cannot see in complete darkness, although they can see better than most mammals in a dim light. The cat in its wild state is a nocturnal animal and does most of its hunting by moonlight. Many nocturnal animals are able to increase the amount of light passing through the retina because they have a reflecting layer in the choroid behind the retina, known as the *tapetum*. The tapetum causes a cat's eyes to shine at night when a bright light is directed at them and this is one of the reasons the cat was regarded as sacred by the Ancient Egyptians. The eyes reflected the sun while it was hidden from Man.

The iris in the cat's eyes is very contractile and is equipped with a dilating muscle which can respond suddenly to light changes. In a dim light, the pupil is widely exposed, allowing the maximum of light to pass through to the retina. In bright light, the opening contracts until the pupil appears as a vertical slit in broad daylight.

The Egyptians and the Chinese associated the cat's eyes with the phases of the moon. Chinese peasants judged the time of day from the eyes of a cat. But this method could only have been reliable when the light was consistently bright at the same time each day.

Cats have a third eyelid called the *nictitating membrane*. This rises from the bottom and inner angle of the orbit and rests upon the eyeball. When a cat is unwell, this third eyelid is plainly visible. Sometimes after severe illness, the membrane stays slightly up but sight is not impaired.

Cats are better able to focus on moving objects than on stationary ones. The eyes are on the front of the head so that distances can be estimated accurately, important for a hunting animal. Cats are colour-blind and see only in shades of black and white.

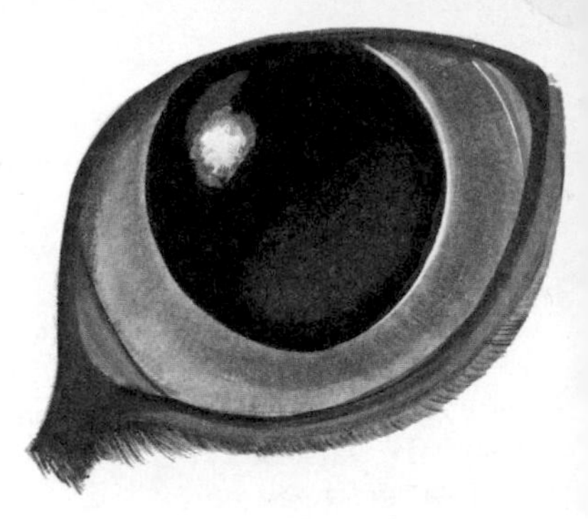

In dim light the pupil is exposed as much as possible to allow the maximum of light to pass to the retina.

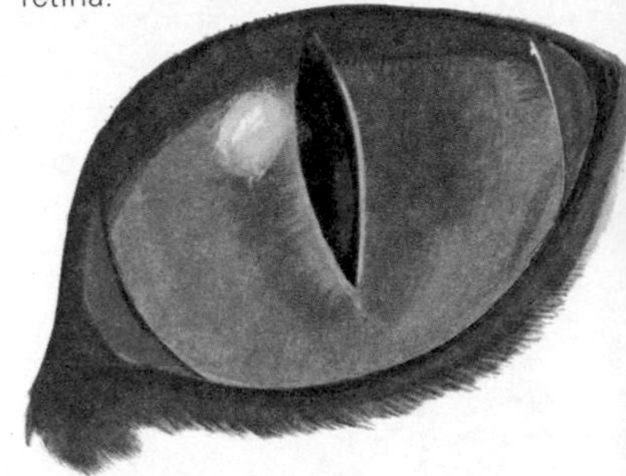

In bright light the pupil narrows to a slit.

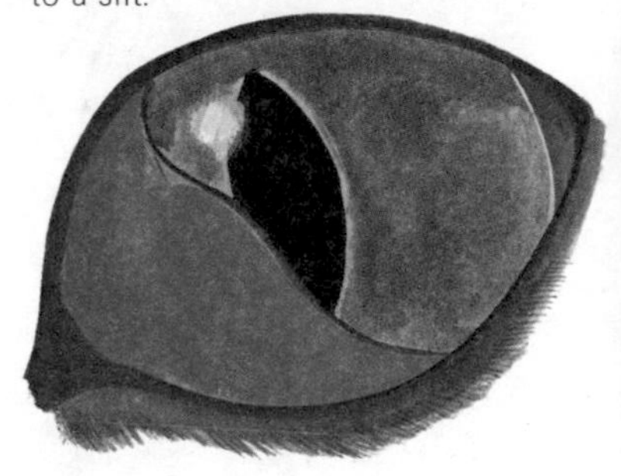

When a cat is unwell the third eyelid, the nictitating membrane, can be seen.

Bone structure

Animals that actively hunt their prey have limbs adapted for sudden leaping movements. Cats are *digitigrade*, which means that they walk on their toes, and the heel-bone is well developed, but set very far back not touching the ground at all. The pads of the foot form cushions which protect the bones on which the weight of the cat rests. Cats have about 230 bones, varying in size and shape.

There are two basic reasons for the remarkable flexibility of the cats body. The first is that the shoulder point is free and open and allows the animal to turn its foreleg in almost any direction without much strain. The second reason is the fact that the collar bone is very small, or in some cats, non-existent. Cats are so finely balanced that their limbs are able to perform rotary movements without danger of dislocation. In fact the entire framework is extremely flexible, which explains why cats are so lithe and agile. The mobility of the spinal column is greatest in the tail, which can be bent freely in any direction.

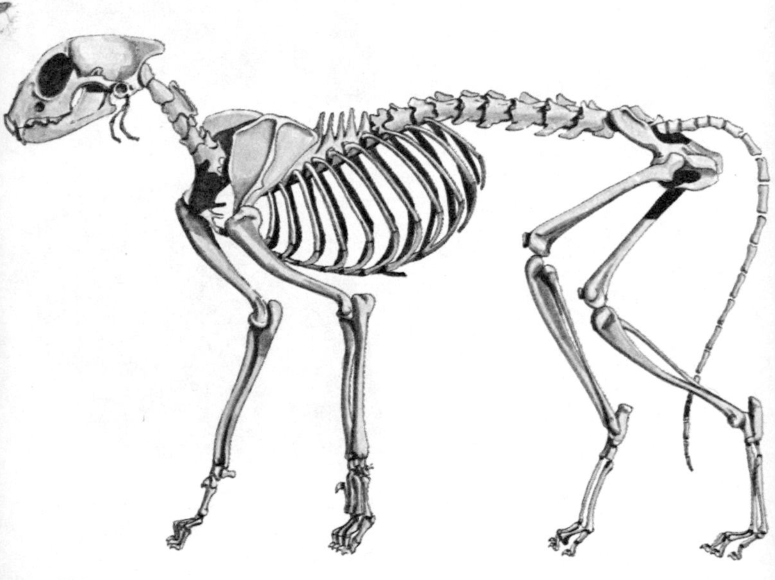

The skeleton is held together by the skeletal muscles, of which there are more than 500. The strongest muscles are to be found in the lumbar region and the hind legs, which are used in springing, and in the neck and shoulders, which are used for striking prey.

Claws

The claws are curved and very sharp, well adapted for the cat to grasp its prey. Cats' claws are retractile, which means they can be extended or retracted by means of flexor tendons. These tendons are elastic ligaments which pass from the root of the claw, through a loop, to the second phalanx. Normally the claws are hidden in openings at the end of the digits, thus remaining sharp for when they are needed. Furthermore when a cat walks, the claws do not scrape on the ground, and betray stealthy movement. The claws on the forefeet can be used independently.

Cats regularly scratch their claws against trees to pull off the outer shells of the claws as they become worn.

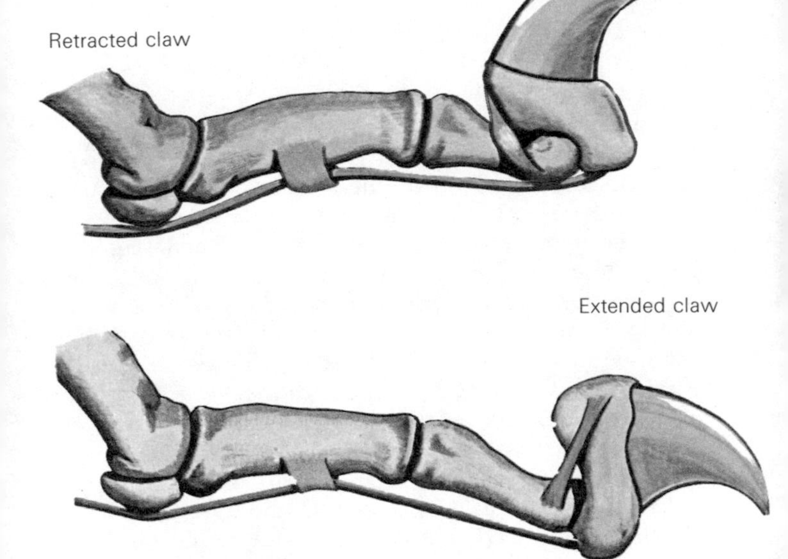

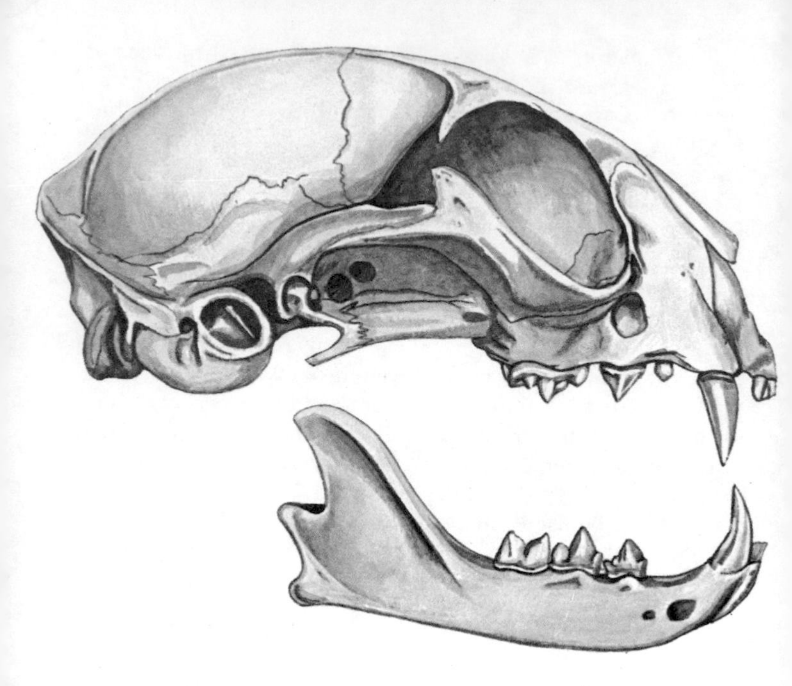

Skull of cat

The jaw

Cats have two sets of teeth: their milk teeth and their adult teeth. When a kitten is about six months old, it sheds its milk teeth. The teeth of an adult cat should be thirty in number. The three front teeth are on either side of a centre line in the upper jaw. They are very small and simple in shape. These front teeth are called *incisors*. Six similar teeth grow in the lower jaw, but they are smaller than the upper incisors. The next tooth in each jaw is a large, strong, conical tooth, somewhat curved and sharply pointed, called the *canine*. Next to the canines are the *premolars*, three of which grow on each side of the upper jaw, and two on each side of the lower jaw. The third premolar is the longest tooth in a cat's jaw. Behind the premolars is an exceedingly small tooth, one on each side of both the upper and lower jaw. These small teeth are the true *molars*. The small size

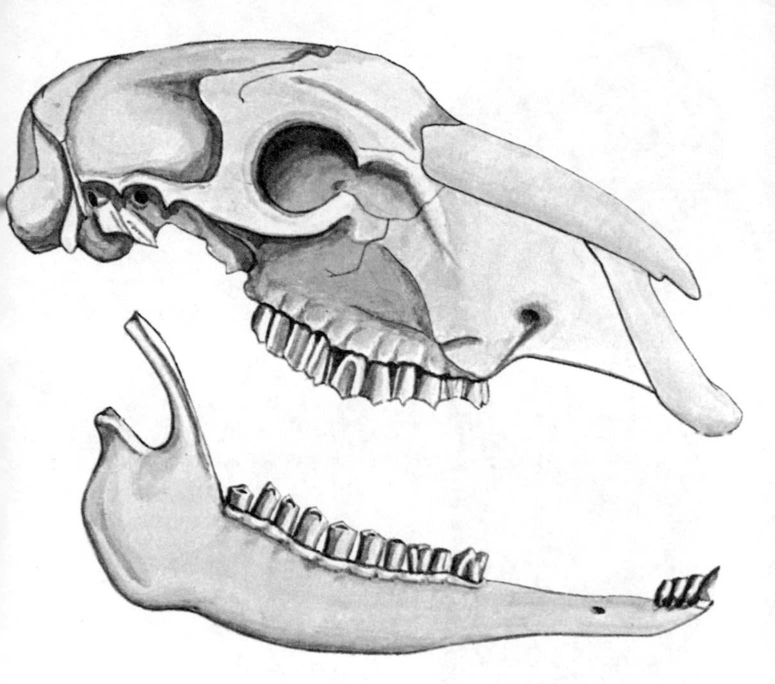

Skull of sheep for comparison

of the incisors allows the canines to penetrate deeply. The last premolar in the upper jaw and the first molar in the lower jaw are sharpened into scissor-like blades.

If the jaws of cats and the jaws of vegetarian animals, such as sheep, are compared it can be found that cats have long sharp teeth with which to catch and kill their prey, and sharp-edged molars which can pare the meat from the bone. Unlike sheep, cats have no flat teeth with which to masticate food.

Movements of the short, powerful jaw are brought about by muscles, the *masseter, temporal* and *pterygoid*. The temporal muscles are used when the lower jaw is raised. Carnivores which have powerful temporal muscles have specially developed skulls, which are adapted to accommodate these exceptionally large muscles. The skulls of all cats are similar and uniform in shape.

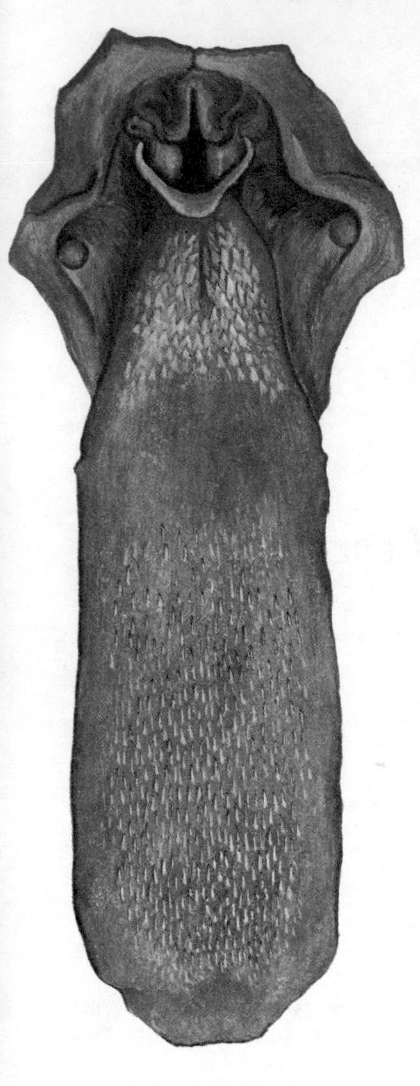

The cat's tongue has almost parallel sides and is long and flat in shape.

The tongue

The tongue of the cat is long and flat with almost parallel sides. It tapers slightly in front and rather more at the back of the mouth. Embedded near the lower surface of the tongue is a spindle-shaped piece of muscular fibre, known as the *lytta* or worm. Scientists believe that this fibre is used in the lapping action. The upper surface of the tongue is covered with rasp-like protuberances called *papillae,* which enable a cat to scrape every piece of meat off a bone and to lick its coat clean. With its tongue, the cat can clean every part of its body, except the exact centre of its back and neck. All over the tongue are taste buds, although there is a particular concentration at the tip and at the very back of the throat. The tongue is also sometimes used as a means of showing affection. Cats are unable to use their lips as organs of touch, unlike many other mammals.

The ears

The cat's hearing is remarkably acute. It can hear high-pitched sounds far beyond the range of the human ear. Extensive tests have shown that, for frequencies below 2,000 cycles per second, the cat responds in very much the same way as Man. Above those frequencies, its hearing is far more sensitive than Man's and it responds to tones of up to 60,000 cycles per second. It has been suggested that a cat's hearing is far more acute than that of a dog and, like many breeds of dog, the cat has a naturally erect ear that helps to catch sounds.

Apart from the special function of hearing, a cat's ear contains various other accessories relative to its well-being. Each ear contains twenty-seven muscles, which enable the part of the ear we can see, known as the *pinna,* to be turned in several directions in order to collect sound waves by means of its prominences and excavations. In the inner ear there are semi-circular canals. A cat's balance depends on them and they play a part in the cat's ability to right itself during a fall. When a cat drops from a height, it always

A falling cat invariably lands on its feet.

The *vibrissae* or whiskers serve as sensitive organs of touch.

manages to land on its feet, because with its strong sense of balance it manages to twist itself round during the fall to make a four-point landing.

The coat

The hair that has almost vanished from the human body covers the cat very thickly. Even the so-called Hairless Cat of Mexico has a fine, almost invisible covering. The only places fur does not grow on a cat's body are the nose, the pads of the feet, the anus and the nipples.

The hairy coat holds a layer of air close to the skin, insulating the body against changes in the outside temperature. Cats, like many mammals, have the protection of an undercoat of fine hair overlaid by longer and coarser guard hairs. The longer hairs sometimes stand on end when the small muscles which pass from the skin to the hair-bulbs contract. This often happens when a cat is enraged and it is quite possible that this is a defence mechanism that the cat has developed to frighten its enemies. A cat with its back arched and fur fluffed up would look like a much more formidable foe.

The skin of a cat is waterproof but it does not prevent the absorption of oils and drugs, which could, if absorbed in a great enough quantity, prove toxic. The skin also contains sweat glands, and so do the pads of the feet. A remarkable quality of the skin is the speed of its regeneration and its ability to fight infection, when the cat has been wounded.

The coat is shed and regrown in spring and autumn. Some hair is longer and grows in tufts which are not shed with the rest. These long-growing hairs are found on the tips of the ears, the eyebrows, and form the cat's whiskers. Such hairs are called the *vibrissae*. They are coarse and feel wiry to the touch. Their special function is to protect the eyes and act as sensitive feelers. The bulbs of these hairs are particularly rich in nerve and blood supply and, as a result, they are very sensitive organs of touch. The idea that domestic cats use their whiskers to test the width of gaps, to see if the body can pass through, is a fallacy. Few overfed pets have whiskers to match their size. However, in poor light this extra sense of touch can be a valuable asset.

The face markings of the tabby

BREEDING CATS

Genetics

Genetics, the science of inheritance, deals with the inborn properties of organisms as distinct from the properties imposed on them by environment. Differences in development are due to the different genes, the ultramicroscopic units of inherited material. Scientists believe that the differences between genetically different strains result from alterations in one or several genes. The changed genes are known as *mutations*. Once a gene has mutated, it is propagated in the altered state. An example of this occurs in the curly coat of the rex cats.

In the development of the kitten, as in all other animals, the genes account for the coat colouring, eye colour, physical characteristics and sex determination. When the gene which controls colour is defective, no colour whatever is produced and the bearer of such genes will be albino.

Albinism is very rare in cats. If you mate an albino cat with a coloured cat, the gene for colour development becomes re-activated and the concealed colour in the albino will reappear in the kittens. Albino cats differ from white cats, because the eyes of the albino show no colour. They have pink eyes and their vision is poor in daytime.

The gene whose influence is most exhibited is known as

the *dominant gene*. The gene which does not show in the presence of the dominant is said to be *recessive*.

Investigations carried out on matings between black and tabby cats strongly support the idea that tabby is dominant to black. Tabby cats can be placed in two classes, the striped tabby, the sides of whose body are marked from shoulder to tail with narrow, vertical stripes, and the blotched tabby, which has longitudinal stripes forming a horseshoe or circular pattern. In matings between striped and blotched tabbies, the striped is dominant.

The tabby's body showing markings on the back and shoulders

The inheritance of black, yellow, and tortoiseshell coat colours amongst cats has produced the most interesting results for geneticists. Whereas all other coat colours are found among males and females alike, the tortoiseshell coat colour is confined almost exclusively to the female. Although an occasional male may appear with this colouring, it is almost invariably sterile.

When mating the *queen* (female) to a stud of the breed of one of the body colours, it is impossible to predict the colour of the kittens. Breeding experiments have shown that black and yellow breed true, yellow being completely dominant over black in the male and incompletely dominant in the female. Thus, in theory, the result of a mating between black and yellow should produce yellow male kittens and tortoiseshell females.

The aim, when breeding for show purposes, is to produce a cat with clear colours, with patching that is not too large and with patterning that extends completely around the body, including the face, ears, legs, paws and tail.

A correlation exists in cats

Below, from left to right: Tortoiseshell, Blue-eyed White and Ginger

between white coats, blue eyes and deafness. White cats with blue eyes are usually deaf, whereas odd-eyed specimens, such as those with one blue eye and one orange eye, appear to have good hearing. Some owners of white cats with this odd-eyed condition believe that the cat can hear only on the side of the orange eye. No evidence supports this view. Blue-eyed, white-haired kittens have been known to be deaf until they are a few months old. The blue eye colour has then changed to orange and the cat has been able to hear.

There is no real explanation for this deafness in white cats. S. Wright, a geneticist working in the 1920s in a study

called *Colour Inheritance in Mammals,* wrote: 'When the white colour is sufficiently intense to invade the eyes it might also invade the inner ear.' He refers to a similar observation of deafness in wall-eyed white dogs.

A normal cat has five toes on each forefoot and four on each hind-foot. It is not uncommon for domestic cats to possess extra toes, a condition that is known as *polydactylism*. The extra digits may occur on both fore and hind-feet, and the number varies from cat to cat. Variations may even occur in two feet of a pair.

Polydactylism has occurred often enough to have been given some attention by geneticists. The geneticists have concluded that the extra toes are a characteristic determined by a dominant gene which may express itself in various ways.

Polydactylism is known to be inherited, but details of the inheritance are unknown. Every degree of abnormality may occur in one litter and will continue through several generations. Irregularity of dominance is exhibited in the way that some families run a perfect course conforming to Mendel's theory,

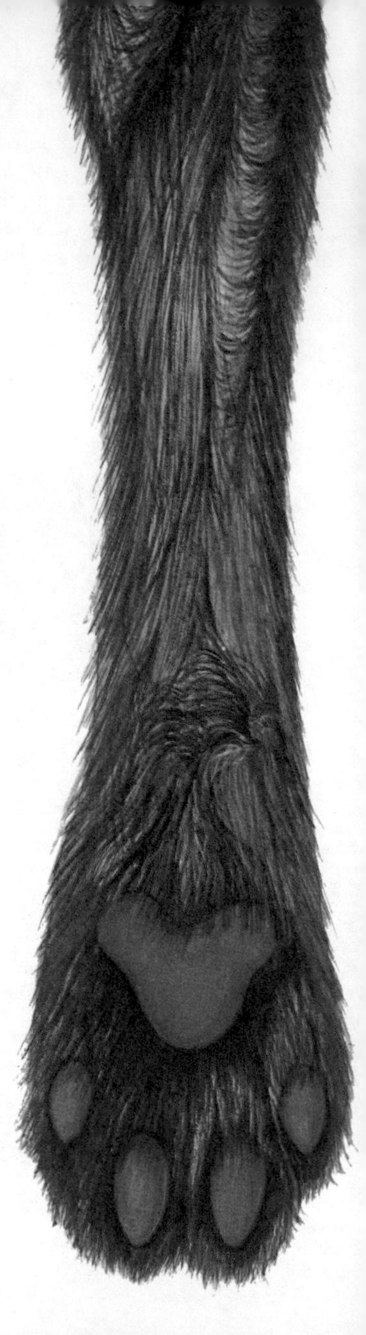

The pads of a normal cat's foot (*left*) and various types of deformity (*above*)

while others produce kittens with normal toes. For example, a cat with a pair of these genes will produce only extra-toed kittens and a cat with only one of these genes, mated to a normal cat, will give extra toes to only half the litter. Two cats, each with one gene for the character, will probably produce twenty-five per cent of their kittens with normal feet. On the other hand similar matings are quite likely to produce kittens with normal toes, although such kittens can transmit extra toes to subsequent generations.

A study of genetics is of prime importance for the breeder of new varieties of cats. Mutations provide the hereditary variation on which selection works.

Rex hair type, for instance, can be transferred to any breed, colour or type of cat. Geneticists and breeders alike believe that the rex coat came about as a mutation involving a single recessive factor. For the breeding of recognized varieties, selection is the key. A kitten gets one half of its characteristics from each of its parents, the grandparents each supply some of their characteristics, as do the earlier generations.

Mating

A female kitten only five months old is often ready to produce her own kittens. Cats first come into season at about this age, and seasons are known as the *mating cycles*. Unlike dogs, which only come into season twice a year, cats do not appear to have a time cycle. Cats may come into season every few weeks during spring and summer, and each cycle may last anything from three days to three weeks. If the female is not mated, it will come into season again almost at once. The cycles continue to occur until the cat is mated, when the cycles will stop.

There is little doubt when a female is in season, because it makes a quite unmistakable noise, known as *calling*. This astonishing sound is a wild cry which can be heard over a great distance. Extreme restlessness is an indication that a cat is about to start calling. It may roll over and over, howling, or rush about making mewing noises. At this time, the female must be kept away from all male cats. Particular care should be taken during the first season, because it is not advisable to let it have kittens at too early an age. But it is not easy to keep it away from the males which take up the challenge of the female's call. It is not unusual to see a tom cat or two, perched on a fence serenading the lady with their eerie caterwauling. A noisy fight followed by the sudden

departure of the vanquished suitor invariably follows.

Fertilization is inevitable under natural conditions, because the queen will be served by all the males present in quick succession. A queen can produce young in one litter that have been fathered by several different males. It is not true that she only conceives from one mating and it is, in fact, possible for every kitten in a litter to have a different father.

When the cat breeder mates his queen, it is one tom to one female. At the first mating a queen is usually rather frightened and that is the reason why an inexperienced cat should always be mated with an experienced one. The artificial conditions of the stud house also impose restrictions such that stud matings are sometimes infertile and to guard against unsuccessful service a second mating should be arranged a day later. Litters from stud matings are frequently smaller in number than those of cats at liberty.

Kittening

Having kittens is a perfectly normal function for a queen. The owner should prepare a bed for the cat in good time. The period of gestation in cats varies between 56 and 69 days, but the average is 62 days – in this too cats are individual. Most cats prefer to have their owners near them at the time their kittens are about to be born, perhaps for reassurance, but nevertheless the owner should be careful not to fuss or try to help when the time comes. Each kitten is born in a sac which the mother will split, cleaning the kitten at the same time. The mother will also eat the placenta. This is natural and stimulates the flow of milk. The birth of the litter may take from two to four hours. If the queen leaves the nest, becomes restless, or is obviously in distress, the best help you can give is to call a veterinary surgeon.

After the kittens have been born, the mother should be left to rest and to care for her family. Light food should be placed close to the nest.

The queen is unlikely to leave her new family for the first few hours and, until she does, no attempt should be made to arrange fresh bedding. It is easier to judge the sexes of the kittens before the fur begins to grow but, apart from such necessary handling, the kittens should not be touched at

Mother cats carry their young by the flap of skin at the back of the neck.

all during the first two days, or the mother may begin to resent the interference. The kittens' eyes are closed but very sensitive to light, and no bright light should be allowed near the nest.

It is necessary to hand rear the kittens when the mother has no milk, or on the rare occasions when the mother dies after the birth of the kittens. Then the babies must be fed every two hours, day and night, after having sought expert advice from a veterinarian. The kittens must be cleaned – a piece of rough towelling will replace the mother's tongue – and they must also be kept warm with a rubber hot-water bottle wrapped in a fluffy blanket.

Sometimes pregnancies are unsuccessful and end in miscarriages, and some are false. Miscarriages can occur without apparent cause, perhaps as a result of disease or mishap. False pregnancies do occur fairly frequently and the cat owner is not able to tell the difference unless the animal is taken to the vet for examination. Usually there is nothing that can be done and the pregnancy must run its full course.

When the mother dies or has no milk, the kittens must be fed by hand.

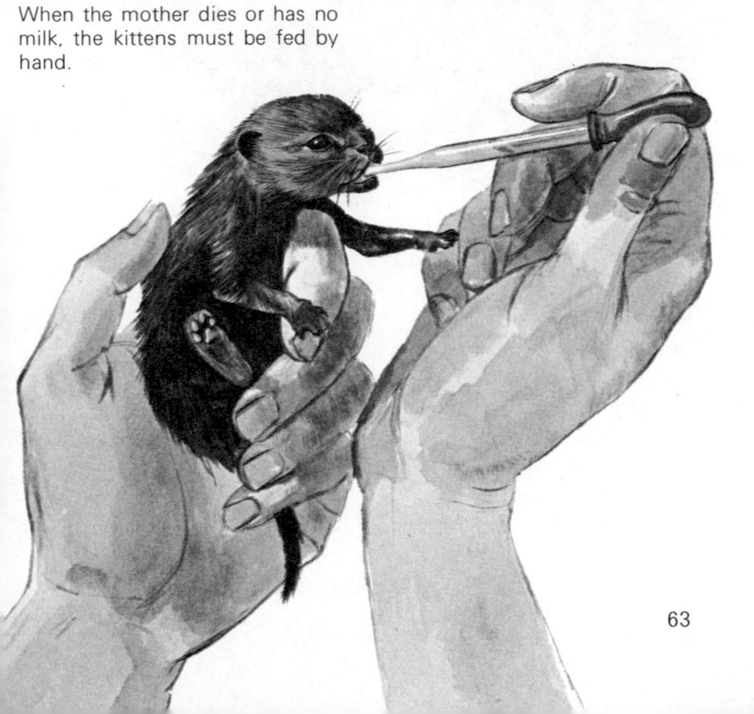

Spaying and neutering

Left to its own devices, a household cat will produce several litters each year. Cats not required for breeding should be neutered at four months and unwanted kittens will be avoided. One of the aims of all cat lovers must be to keep the cat population within reasonable limits. Each year, far too many cats are sent to clinics for destruction. It is better to have a few well-cared-for cats than many that are left to fend for themselves.

Cat owners can help to achieve this objective by having all tom kittens neutered when they are between three and five months old. Fully-grown cats can be operated on with a minimum of risk and a neutered cat is less likely to stray and is often more contented. The operation by which the female is neutered is called *spaying*. It involves the removal of the ovaries, and is therefore a bigger operation than the neutering of the male. An early age is recommended for females although the fact that a cat has already had kittens need be no deterrent, because the operation can be performed at any age. In all cases of neutering, the work must be undertaken by a veterinary surgeon.

Unwanted kittens

An un-neutered female will probably produce so many kittens that it will become difficult to find good homes for them. Female kittens are especially difficult to place. In the past, unwanted kittens have often been drowned, but this is heartless and cruel. If they are to be destroyed, then it must be done at birth, either by a veterinary surgeon or by another experienced person. When no kittens are to be kept, the mother should, immediately after birth, be given two teaspoonfuls of salad oil mixed with sardine oil. A light diet containing no meat should be given for the first four or five days, with milk or water to drink.

Unwanted kittens should not be turned out to become strays.

Breeding for the show

Breeding to type is the aim of every breeder of pedigree cats. The art of the breeder lies in careful selection. For example, the more good points the parents possess in common, the more likely they are to produce kittens which are good specimens. The Mendelian law of inheritance must be remembered. Characteristics are passed not only from the parents, but from earlier generations. The small breeder would be unwise to keep a stud cat of his own, because, for obvious reasons, the cat cannot be kept in constant company with the females. If a stud cat were limited to only a few females, it would become noisy and bad-tempered, and even savage.

In Britain, the Governing Council of the Cat Fancy publish a stud list every year. This list helps British breeders to select a stud for their pedigree queens. In the United States, a number of cat societies advise breeders. The British list gives the names and addresses of owners of stud toms,

together with the fees payable. Arrangements should be made in advance, so that only a telephone call to the owner of the stud is needed when next the queen *calls* (comes into season). It should be taken to the stud on the second day of calling. The queen must be conveyed carefully in a warm basket or suitable box. The basket or box must be clearly marked indicating that it contains livestock.

Some breeders believe that one mating with a proved sire should be sufficient. But others allow for a second mating in case the first was unsuccessful. Most owners allow a second visit when there are no results from the first visit. Such arrangements are private and the owner is under no obligation to allow it.

On the return from the stud the queen must not mix with other males for at least a week. It must be remembered that it is quite possible for a cat to produce kittens from one or more mating in one litter.

BREEDS OF CATS

British short-haired breeds

With one exception, all short-haired breeds are either British short-hairs or foreign short-hairs. The one exception to the rule is the Manx Cat, which differs from all the other cats because it has no tail. In every other respect, however, it is British in type.

The body of the British short-hair cat should be well-

British short-hair type

knit and powerful. It should have good depth, with a full, broad chest. The tail should be thick at the base and well set with its length in proportion to the body. The legs should be strong and well-proportioned with neat, well-rounded feet. The head should be broad between the ears, the cheeks well developed, and the face and nose short. The coat should be short, fine and close. All British short-hairs are awarded a maximum of 50 points for these standard, leaving 50 points to be apportioned for colour and eyes in the individual breeds.

Foreign short-hair type

The scale of points for these cats is:

Body and tail	10
Legs and feet	5
Head and neck	10
Ears	10
Coat	10
Condition	5
Total	50

The fact that only five points are awarded for condition does not mean that this particular point is not considered of much importance by show judges. It is in fact the most important feature to be considered and a cat out of condition will not win points. A judge is most likely to assume that a cat that is not in condition is not up to the required show standard and will not consider the other points very closely.

Foreign short-haired breeds

The body of the foreign short-hair should be lightly built, long and lissom. The head should be long and wedge-shaped, wide at the top and narrowing to a fine muzzle. The eyes should be almond-shaped and the ears large, being wide at the base and pointed and pricked. Keeping the balance, the tail should be thin and whipped, long, and tapering to a point at the tip. The scales of points are given with the descriptions of the particular breeds.

Long-haired breeds

Many people consider long-haired cats to be the most beautiful of all. Generally known as Persian cats, they first appeared in Europe towards the end of the sixteenth century. The varieties differ in colouring, but the standards require them to have a long flowing coat, fine in texture, glossy, and standing off from the body. The immense ruff should continue in a deep frill between the front legs. The tail should be short and full. The head should show great breadth of skull, with small, neat and well covered ears, a short nose, full cheeks and a broad muzzle. The body should be cobby and massive, and the legs should be short and thick.

Long-haired cats are usually known as Persians. Standards require that they have a long, fine, glossy coat, the ruff continuing in a deep frill between the front legs and the tail short and full.

Long-haired Blacks

The Long-haired Black is one of the oldest long-haired breeds to be shown in Britain. The colour must be lustrous, raven-black to the roots, and free from rustiness, shading, white hairs or markings of any kind. To achieve perfection when breeding, it is wise to introduce one of the Long-haired Blues into the line occasionally to improve the type. Black to Black breeding will produce Black kittens, but there will be a deterioration in type. The majority of the Long-haired Black champions have one Blue Long-hair in the pedigree. Eye colour is important. The eyes should be large, round and wide open, and coloured copper or deep orange, with no green rim. It is difficult to eradicate the green rim and perhaps this is responsible for the scarcity of good Long-haired Blacks today.

In the Official Standards of Points, published by the Governing Council of the Cat Fancy, we are told that the kittens 'are often a very bad colour up to five or six months, their coats being grey or rusty in parts, and sometimes freely speckled with white hairs. Fanciers should not condemn them on this account if good in other respect, as these kittens frequently turn into the densest Blacks.' The Governing Council of the British Cat Fancy awards points as follows: colour 25; coat 20; body 20; head 20; eyes 15.

The American Cat Fanciers' Association allocates the following points: head 10; ears 5; body 15; tail 5; legs and feet 10; eye opening 5; eye colour 5; coat 15; colour 20; condition and balance 10.

The body shape of the Long-haired Black is the same for all varieties. It is described as cobby, which means short

and thick, in cat fanciers' language. The neck should be strong, shoulders broad and flat. There should be plenty of bone and substance. The legs should be short and the body finished off with a short, well-plumed tail.

The long coat calls for constant attention. Without it, the coat will become tangled and felted, and as a result the health of the cat will suffer. For special occasions, such as the show, the coat can be polished with a piece of silk or chamois leather.

Long-haired Black

Kittens may have tabby markings which disappear after about 5 to 6 months. Standards are so high that the Governing Council of the British Cat Fancy advises members not to enter their cats for show if they do not come up to the requirements.

Long-haired Blues

The standard is high for this beautiful cat. Any shade of blue is allowed, but the colour must be even all over. White hairs, shadings or markings are serious faults.

The body should be cobby and the shoulders at the withers should be broad and flat. The chest should be broad and rounded and the hips the same width as the shoulders. The short, thick legs must be well-furnished, and the tail short and full. The lovely, wide eyes should be deep orange or copper-coloured without a trace of green. If a horizontal line is taken across the top of the head, it should touch only the tips of the ears. The ears should be small and set well down at either side of the skull. The head is required to be broad with well-rounded contours, and the nose should be broad and snub. The female is generally smaller and must look feminine.

Standards for Long-haired Blues

Coat: any shade of blue allowable, sound and even in colour; free from markings, shadings, or any white hairs. Fur long, thick, and soft in texture. Frill full.

Head: broad and round, with width between the ears. Face and nose short. Ears small and tufted. Cheeks well-developed.

Eyes: deep orange or copper; large, round and full, without trace of green.

Body: cobby and low on the legs.

Tail: short and full, not tapering (a kink shall be considered a defect).

Scale of points: coat 20; condition 10; head 25; eyes 20; body 15; tail 10.

Red Self
Long-hair
Red Tabby
Long-hair

Red Tabby Long-hairs

The deep orange ground colour of the Red Tabby is marked with rich bands in a pattern similar to that of the Brown Tabby. The markings are most important, as with all coloured tabbies. They must be clearly and boldly defined, continuing on down the chest, legs and tail. The tail must not end in a white tip and care should be taken not to use a cat with this fault for breeding, because it is almost certain to reappear in a generation or two. The white tip seems to be one of the hardest faults to breed out. It is a simple matter for the breeder to weed out undesirables at once and rear only the best of the litter for show purposes, because unlike many breeds, the kittens show their markings clearly from birth.

The eyes should be deep orange or copper. After each season of service, some deterioration of the eye colour occurs and, for this reason, matings should be restricted. Difficulty seems to be experienced in breeding a good Red Tabby. Tall ears and narrow heads tend to occur more often than in the majority of long-haired cats. These features are considered bad faults.

In the Cat Fancy of the United States, the Peke-faced Persian is a popular breed which is exhibited under the Red and Red Tabby classes.

Standards for Red Tabby Long-hairs

Colour and markings: deep, rich, red colour, markings to be clearly defined, continuing on down the chest, legs and tail.

Coat: long, dense and silky; short and flowing tail with no white tip.

Body: cobby and solid, with short, thick legs.

Head: broad and round. Small ears, well-set and well-tufted. Short, broad nose. Full, round cheeks.

Eyes: large and round, deep copper colour.

Scale of points: coat 50; body 15; head 20; eyes 15.

Red Self Long-hairs

A perfect Red Self is seldom seen. The colour must be a deep, rich, clear red, free from shadings, markings or tickings. When the fur is parted, it must show the same density of colour at the roots as at the tip. Such perfection is difficult to achieve. More often than not tabby markings appear.

Standards for Red Self Long-hairs
Colour: deep, rich red, without markings.
Coat: long, dense and silky; tail short and flowing.
Body: cobby and solid, with short, thick legs.
Head: broad and round. Small ears, well-set and well-tufted. Short broad nose. Full, round cheeks.
Eyes: large and round, deep copper colour.
Scale of points: the same as those given for the Red-Tabby.

Long-haired Creams

The lovely Long-haired Cream is becoming a popular rival to the Blue Long-hair. The Long-haired Cream is a most attractive breed. The colour, a rich, slightly warm-toned ivory, is most important. It is said that the breed sprang from an early mating of a Blue male with a Red female. Breeders now endeavour to keep away from the Red, because the reddish colours tends to return to the coat and when this happens, the experts describe it as *hot*. The hot-cream colour is a definite fault, because the aim of the breeder is to produce a pale, clear colour, and each hair must be coloured the same from the tip to the root. The body colour should be consistent, and the undersides

The Long-haired Cream, showing the deep copper eye colour

should be as cream as the back and sides. To keep this cool colour it has been found helpful to breed with a Blue male.

Eyes are a special feature in the Cream Long-hair. They must be large and round. The deep copper colour required gives a beautiful contrast to the coat colour. The tail should be short and flowing. Good grooming is essential and very rewarding, because the coat is this cat's magnificent feature. The frill should extend like a halo around the head. The texture should be soft and silky. It should be shiny, alive-looking, and standing away from the body.

Standards for Long-haired Creams

Colour: to be pure and sound throughout, without shadings or markings.

Coat: long, dense and silky; tail short and flowing.

Body: cobby and solid, with short, thick legs.

Head: broad and round. Small ears, well-set and well-tufted. Short, broad nose. Full, round cheeks.

Eyes: large and round, deep copper colour.

Scale of points: colour (pale to medium) 30; coat condition 20; body 15; head 20; eyes 15.

Long-haired Smokes

Long-haired Smokes are now quite rare. The breed is obtained by crossing Blue-Chinchillas with Blacks. This produces Smokes and Blue-Smokes. The kittens are born black or blue, and the white undercoat begins to show when the kittens are about three weeks old. No signs of tabby markings or blue undercoat should appear.

A Smoke is a cat of contrasts. The undercolour should be as white as possible, with the tips shading to black. The dark points should be most defined on the back, head and feet, and the light points on the frill, flanks and ear tufts.

Standards for Long-haired Smokes

Colour of body: black, shading to silver on sides, flanks, and mask.

Feet: black, with no markings. *Frill and ear tufts:* silver. *Undercolour:* as nearly white as possible.

Coat and condition: silky texture, long and dense, extra-long frill.

Shape of head: broad and round, with width between the ears. Snub nose. *Ears:* small and tufted.

Body: cobby, not coarse, but massive, short legs.

Eyes: orange or copper in colour, large and round in shape. pleasing expression.

Brush: short and bushy.

Scale of points: colour 40; coat and condition 20; shape 20; eyes 10; brush 10.

The standard is the same for Blue-Smokes, except that the word 'black' should be substituted throughout for 'blue'. The standard set by the British Cat Fanciers Association for Smokes is the same as for all Persians. Objections are made to pale eye colour.

Long-haired Tortoiseshells

The number of Tortoiseshell Long-hairs is small because, when mating the queen with a stud of one of the body colours, it is not possible to forecast the colour of the kittens. The makeup consists of three colours – black, red and cream. The patches must be well broken and spread over the whole body, especially on the face. A Tortoiseshell cat is almost always female. When a male does appear, it is invariably sterile.

Long-haired Smoke

Long-haired Tortoiseshell

Few Tortoiseshells conform closely to the standards. It is difficult to achieve a red that is dark enough, or one that carries the required patching in equal quantities. A Tortoiseshell would be faulted for bearing tabby markings, stripes or bars, and for having solid colour on the face, legs or tail.

Standards for Long-haired Tortoiseshells

Colour: three colours, black, red, and cream, well broken into patches; colours to be bright and rich, well broken on the face.

Coat: long and flowing, extra long on frill and brush.

Body: cobby and massive, with short legs.

Head: round and broad. Small well-placed and well-tufted ears. Short, broad nose. Full, round cheeks.

Eyes: large and round, deep orange or copper.

Scale of points: coat 50; body 15; head 20; eyes 15.

Long-haired Tortoiseshell-and-Whites

The three colours of the Long-haired Tortoiseshell-and-White are interspersed with white. New Englanders call this breed the Calico Cat. The American Cat Fanciers' Association require the white markings to be limited to certain areas, so that the cat looks as if it had been dropped into a can of white paint.

Standards for Long-haired Tortoiseshell-and-Whites

Colour: the three colours, black, red, and cream, to be well-broken and interspersed with white.

Coat: long and flowing, extra long on brush and frill.

Body: cobby and massive, with short legs.

Head: round and broad. Small, well-tufted ears. Short, broad nose. Full, round cheeks.

Eyes: large and round, deep orange or copper.

Scale of points: coat 50; body 15; head 20; eyes 15.

Long-haired Tortoise-shell-and-White

Blue-eyed White Long-hairs

There are two breeds of White Long-haired Cats recognized by the Governing Council of the British Cat Fancy – White with blue eyes and White with orange eyes. The American Cat Fanciers' Association recognizes a third, the Odd-eyed White, which has one blue eye and one orange.

The eye colour is difficult to achieve. A breeder cannot be sure of getting the deep sapphire-blue required, and although kittens may be born with the necessary depth of colour, they may well have green eyes when adult. Blue-eyed White Long-hairs are not easy to breed, and there are comparatively few of them. The kittens are often delicate and most suffer from the deafness which seems to accompany blue eyes.

Standards for Blue-eyed White Long-hairs

Colour: pure white without marks or shade of any kind.

Coat: long and flowing on body, full frill and brush which should be short and broad; the coat should be close, soft and silky, not woolly in texture.

Body: cobby and massive, without being coarse, with plenty of bone substance, and low on the leg.

Head: round and broad, with plenty of space between the ears, which should be small. Neat and well-covered, short nose. Full cheeks and broad muzzle.

Eyes: large, round and wide-open, deep blue in colour.

Head of the Orange-eyed White (*left*), and the Blue-eyed White Long-hair (*opposite*)

Orange-eyed White Long-hairs

In 1938, the Governing Council of the British Cat Fancy granted challenge certificates to White Long-hairs with orange eyes as a separate entry. They had formerly been judged in one class along with those having blue eyes. Since the Orange-eyed White invariably was of a better type, it had the advantage until it became a separate breed.

The same points are awarded as for the Blue-eyed White, except for eye colour, which should be orange or copper.

Whites are prone to yellow stains on their tails, caused by accumulated dust and grease. Owners should carefully attend to this very damaging peculiarity and remove any stains before showing the cat.

Scale of points for White Long-hairs: colour 25; coat 20; body 20; head 20; eyes 15.

Blue-Cream Long-hair

Blue-Cream Long-hairs

In order to obtain this beautiful breed, a Cream female should be mated to a Blue male. The resulting kittens will be Cream males and Blue-Cream females. Males of this variety are rare and, like the Tortoiseshell males, they are apt to be sterile. The standard aimed at in Britain and in the rest of Europe is for a coat with softly intermingled colours, giving a soft, misty appearance. Much work has been done to eliminate the small patches of blue or cream which frequently occur on the legs, face or head. But it is not easy to achieve the lovely pastel shades with the desired intermingling of colour.

In the United States, the Blue-Cream is recognized under the Tortoiseshell or 'Tortie' division. The two colours, clear blue and cream, should be arranged to conform to the Tortoiseshell standard. Undesirable features are brindled colours, tabby markings, stripes and bars, and solid colour on the legs, face or tail. This variety does occur in Britain but it is not now officially recognized, although for many years the English Blue-Cream was patched.

Standards for Blue-Cream Long-hairs

Colour and markings: to consist of blue and cream, softly intermingled, pastel shades.

Coat: to be dense and very soft and silky.

Head and type: head broad and round. Tiny ears, well-placed and well-tufted. Short, broad nose. Colour intermingled on face.

Eyes: deep copper or orange.

Body: short, cobby and massive, with short, thick legs.

Scale of points: colour 30; coat and condition 20; head and type 20; eyes 15; body 15.

Brown Tabby Long-hairs

It is not easy to produce a Long-haired Brown Tabby with the correct marking. The classic tabby marking must conform to a definite pattern. The ground colour and the deep heavy marking must be well contrasted. The head must be barred, with frown marks extending between the ears and down the neck to meet the *butterfly* on the shoulders. The pattern should continue from the back, under the body, and join in the middle of the stomach.

Brown Tabby Long-hair and
Silver Tabby Long-hair

Standards for Brown Tabby Long-hairs
Colour and markings: rich, tawny sable, with delicate, black pencillings running down the face. Cheeks crossed with two or three distinct swirls. The chest crossed by two narrow, unbroken lines, with butterfly markings on shoulders.
Coat: long and flowing; tail short and full.
Body: cobby and massive, with short legs.
Head: round and broad. Small well-placed and well-tufted ears. Short, broad nose. Full, round cheeks.
Eyes: large and round, hazel or copper colour.
Scale of points: coat 50; body 15; head 20; eyes 15.

Silver Tabby Long-hairs

As with all tabby long-hairs good specimens are not easily obtained, because the long hair rather obscures the markings. In this breed, the brown ground colour of the Brown Tabby is replaced by a pure pale silver. Unfortunately this colour is

often brindled and grey, and a rusty tinge can be seen in the black. Breeding for blue-green eyes has led to deterioration in type, although recently there has been renewed interest in the breed and some excellent examples are now exhibited.

Standards for Silver Tabby Long-hairs

Colour: ground colour pure pale silver, with decided jet-black markings, any brown tinge being a drawback.

Head: broad and round, with breadth between the ears, and wide at muzzle. Short nose. Small, well-tufted cars.

Shape: cobby body, with short, thick legs.

Eyes: green or hazel.

Coat and condition: silky in texture, long and dense, extra long on frill.

Tail: short and bushy.

Scale of points: colour 40; head 20; shape 10; tail 5; eyes (green or hazel) 10; coat and condition 15.

Chinchillas

The Chinchilla is one of the loveliest of all cats and in every way it must appear ethereal with no coarseness. The beauty of the Chinchilla lies in its colouring. It is said to have originated from a crossing of Tortoiseshell with Silver Tabby. The kittens demonstrate their ancestry, because they are always born with tabby rings on the tail and often are heavily marked all over. As they grow, such markings gradually disappear. The best adult specimens are those with a pure white undercoat, each hair tipped with black to give a sparkling, silver appearance. This tipping must be evenly-distributed over the shoulders, back, flanks, head and tail.

The American Cat Fanciers' Association also recognizes the Shaded Silver, which has an undercoat that is more grey than white. The top of the head, the shoulders, and back are dark, shading to white on the undersides and legs. Where the Chinchilla appears as silver, the Shaded Silver looks more like pewter. The Masked Silver resembles the Silver but the face is masked with very dark colour, and the paws are also dark.

Standards for Chinchillas

Colour: the undercoat should be pure white, the coat on the back, flanks, head, ears and tail being tipped with black; this tipping to be evenly distributed giving the characteristic sparkling appearance. The legs may be very slightly shaded with the tipping, but the chin, ear tufts, stomach and chest must be pure white; any tabby markings or brown or cream tinge are drawbacks. The tip of the nose should be brick-red, and the visible skin on the eyelids and pads should be black or dark brown.

Head: broad and round, with breadth between the ears, and wide at the muzzle. Snub nose. Small, well-tufted ears.

Shape: cobby body, with short, thick legs.

Eyes: large, round and most expressive, emerald or blue-green in colour.

Coat and condition: silky and fine in texture, long and dense, extra long on the frill.

Tail: short and bushy.

Scale of points: colour 25; head 20; shape 15; eyes 15; coat and condition 15; tail 10.

Chinchilla

Colourpoint Long-hairs

The Colourpoint Long-hair is one of the more recent British breeds. It first received official recognition from the British Governing Council of the Cat Fancy in 1955, and is each year growing in popularity.

Breeders in several countries experimented over a long period with various crossings in an attempt to obtain a Long-haired Siamese. Experiments in the United States continued until the Second World War, but the new variety was not satisfactory because the Siamese cat is the wrong shape to look attractive with long hair. The smooth elegance, which is the great attraction of the Siamese, was concealed by the coat.

In Britain experiments were continued along similar lines with the aim of eliminating the Siamese type. The new Long-haired Siamese were mated to the best possible Persians in order to transfer the Siamese colouring to the Persian body shape. The size and colour of the eyes still presents difficulties to the breeders, because these cats tend to have pale blue eyes. The ideal specimen carries the lovely sapphire-blue colour of the eyes of the Siamese, combined with the large, round shape of the eyes of the Persian. Any similarity in type between this cat and the Siamese is now considered by the

Colourpoint Long-hair

British Governing Council of the Cat Fancy to be most undesirable and incorrect.

Standards for Colourpoint Long-hairs

Coat: fur long, thick and soft in texture, frill full. Colour to be seal, lilac, blue, or chocolate-pointed with appropriate body colour as for Siamese, that is, cream, glacial white, ivory, or magnolia respectively. Points to be of solid colour, and body shading, if any, to tone with the points.

Head: broad and round, with width between the ears. Face and nose short. Ears small and tufted. Cheeks well-developed.

Eyes: shape, large, round and full. Colour, clear, bright and decidedly blue.

Body: cobby and low on leg.

Tail: short and full, not tapering (a kink shall be considered a defect).

Note: any similarity in type to Siamese to be considered most undesirable and incorrect.

Scale of points: coat 15; point and body colour 10; head 30; shape of eye 10; colour of eye 10; body 15; tail 10.

Short-haired Blacks

Owing to the superstitions attached to black cats, people tend to think that they are common. In fact the vast numbers of black, household cats are very rarely completely black, and they almost always have green eyes. The Black Cat bred for the show must have jet-black hair with no trace of rustiness. Its eyes must be orange with no trace of green, even in the rims. This breed has been obtained by long years of tabby crossings. In the kittens, faint stripes are almost always seen, but they usually disappear. The standards given by the British Governing Council of the Cat Fancy are the same for all British short-hairs (page 68). Half the remaining points are apportioned for colour and half for eyes in the individual breeds.

Standards for Short-haired Blacks

Colour: jet-black to the roots, with no rusty tinge and no white hairs anywhere.

Eyes: large, round and well-opened. Colour deep copper or orange with no trace of green.

Scale of points: general short-hair standard 50; colour 25; eyes 25.

Short-haired Whites, Blue and Orange-eyed

Very few White Short-hairs are exhibited at shows. Blue eyes and white colouring usually indicate deafness. A newer, still uncommon, breed is the Orange-eyed White.

The standard for both breeds only differs in eye colour. The coat colour must be white, untinged with yellow, and the eyes must be very deep, sapphire-blue, or golden-orange or copper.

British Blues

Perhaps the most popular of all the short-hairs is the British Blue. It is a striking animal, with its lovely, lavender coat and amber eyes. Formerly its colour was dark slate or plum-blue, but such colours have been bred out. Successful efforts are now being made to improve the coat, because the coat suffered as a result of various crossings made with Russian Blues, and Blue Long-hairs, which were an attempt to improve the eye colour. Each hair on the coat must be

Short-haired White and Short-haired Black

uniform in colour, blue from tip to roots, and the entire body must be of one unbroken colour.

The French have a breed, called the Chartreux, which is very similar to the British Blue. The French standard for the Chartreux requires a coat of any shade of grey or greyish-blue. The British standards are those general for all short-hairs.

Standards for British Blues

Colour: light to medium blue, very level in colour, with no tabby markings, shading, or white anywhere.

Eyes: large and full, copper, orange, or yellow.

Scale of points: general standard 50; colour 25; eyes 25.

The American Cat Fanciers' Association recognizes a blue cat which is sometimes called Maltese. The show standards for this cat require the lightest colour possible.

Cream Short-hairs and Blue-Cream Short-hairs

The Cream Short-hair, a very pale red cat, is rare at shows. Its colour must be rich cream, level, and free from bars, with no sign of white. 25 points are awarded for colour, and 25 for large full eyes, coloured copper or hazel.

Blue-Cream Short-hairs are a more recent variety. The British show standard requires the hairs to be mingled, but the standards in the United States require that the coat be patched.

Standards for Blue-Cream Short-hairs
Eyes: copper, orange, or yellow (not green).
Coat: colours to be softly mingled, not patched, and short and fine in texture.
Scale of points: type as for British cats 40; colour (mingling) 35; eyes 20; condition 5.

Left to right: Blue-Cream Short-hair, Cream Short-hair and British Blue.

Tortoiseshell Short-hairs

Tortoiseshell Short-hairs are known in the United States as Spanish Cats, Calimanco Cats and Clouded Tigers. Males are extremely scarce and invariably sterile. For breeding, the stud should be a Self, which has one of the coat colours. The coats of Tortoiseshell Long-hairs tend to obscure the markings. The standard for the Short-hair requires more clearly defined markings. Well-marked Tortoiseshells showing no tabby markings are rare.

Standards for Tortoiseshell Short-hairs

The general standard for all Short-hairs applies to this breed, 50 points being awarded for body shape, ears, coat and condition.

Tortoiseshell-and-White Short-hair

Colour: black and red (light and dark), equally balanced, and each colour to be as brilliant as possible, no white. Patches to be clear and defined, no blurring, and no tabby or brindle markings. Legs, feet, tail and ears to be as well patched as the body and head. Red blaze desirable – 35 points.
Eyes: orange, copper, or hazel – 15 points.

Tortoiseshell-and-White Short-hairs

Japanese sailors believe that their Tortoiseshell-and-White Short-hairs bring them luck, by preventing shipwreck, and keep away the spirits of the deep.

The colour of these cats, for which they are awarded 35 points, should be black and red (dark and light), on white, and equally balanced. Colours should be brilliant and free from brindling or tabby markings. Tricolour patching should cover the top of the head, ears, cheeks, back, tail and part of the flanks. Patches should be clear and defined and a white blaze is desirable.

No rule can be laid down for the patching of this breed but it should be remembered that white must never predominate and the reverse is on the whole preferable. Eyes (15 points) should be orange, copper or hazel. All structural points should follow those given for Black Cats.

Tortoiseshell Short-hair

Varieties of Short-hair Tabby and Spotted Cats

The two basic tabby patterns are striped and blotched. Both patterns never occur on one cat. The blotched pattern results from a dominant colour gene over striped. In all tabby cats, the tail must be neatly ringed, and chest ring or rings are most desirable – almost essential.

Brown Tabby Cat markings should be very dense and black, not mixed with the ground colour, and quite distinct from it. Ground colour should be rich sable or brown, uniform throughout with no white (35 points). Eyes should be orange, hazel, deep yellow or green (15 points).

Silver Tabby Cat markings should be dense black, not mixed with the ground colour, and quite distinct from it. Ground colour should be pure, clear silver, uniform throughout with no white anywhere (35 points). Eyes should be round and well-opened, coloured green or hazel (15 points).

Red Tabby Cat markings should be very dense and dark red, not mixed with the ground colour, and quite distinct from it. Ground colour and markings should be as rich as possible (35 points). Eyes should be hazel or orange (15 points).

Brown Tabby

Silver Tabby

Spotted Cat

Mackerel-striped Tabby

(*Bottom*) Red Tabby

Mackerel-striped Tabby Cat markings should be as dense as possible, distinct from the ground colour. Rings should be as narrow and numerous as possible, running vertically from the spine towards the ground (35 points). Eyes should be of a colour conforming to the coat pattern (15 points). **Spotted Cats** must have good, clear spotting. The spots may be of any colour suitable to the ground colour. The fewer stripes the better. 50 points should be allotted to spotting and the remaining 50 to the ordinary short-haired properties.

The ideal Russian Blue Short-hair should present a snake-like appearance.

Russian Blue Short-hairs

This foreign short-hair did not originate in Russia, although at one time it was known as the Archangel Cat and numerous legends associate it with Russia. The first Russian Blue to be exported to the United States from Britain, in 1900, had amber eyes. Since that time, the eye colour has been altered and now the requirements are for vivid green eyes.

Standards for Russian Blue Short-hairs

Colour: bright blue, even throughout, and free from tabby markings or shadings; medium to dark shade of blue.

Coat: very short, close, and lustrous, and of sealskin texture.

Body, build, and tail: body long, lithe, graceful in outline and carriage, tail fairly long and tapering. The legs are longish, and the feet small, neat and well-rounded.

Head and neck: the skull is flat and narrow, the forehead receding, giving a wedge-shaped effect. The face and neck are long, giving the long, lithe body.

Eyes: set rather wide apart, of vivid green colour.

Ears: rather large, wide at the base, with very little inside furnishing; skin of the ear thin and transparent, and not too thickly covered with hair. The tips of the ears should be pointed rather than round.

Faults: white markings; tabby markings; cobby or heavy build; square head.

Scale of points: colour 25; coat 25; body, build and tail 15; ears 5; eyes 15; head and neck 15.

Bi-coloured Cats

The colour (20 points) should be black and white, blue and white, orange and white, or cream and white. There should be no tabby shadings in the self-coloured portion. The black, blue, orange, or cream marking (25 points) should start immediately behind the shoulders round the barrel of the body. It should include the tail and hind legs, leaving the hind feet white. The ears and mask of the face should also be self-coloured. The shoulders should be white, also the neck, forelegs and feet, chin, lips and blaze up the face and over the top of the head, joining or running into the white at the back of the skull, thus dividing the mask exactly in half. The eyes (5 points) should be copper, orange or amber.

Manx Cats

Tailless cats live in many parts of the world and there seems to be no evidence to support the belief that the Manx Cat originated from the Isle of Man. Taillessness, height of hind-quarters, shortness of back, and depth of flank are essentials in a Manx Cat. Only a combination of these feature gives the cat its true rabbity or hopping gait, a factor of primary importance. The coat is described as *double*, that is, soft and open, like that of a rabbit, with a soft, thick undercoat, another essential feature. Great attention should also be paid to roundness of rump, ideally as round as an orange.
Scale of points: taillessness 15; height of hind-quarters 15; shortness of back 15; roundness of rump 10; depth of flank 10; double coat 10; head and ears 10; colour and markings 5; eyes 5; condition 5.

Taillessness must be absolute in a show specimen. There

Taillessness must be absolute in a show specimen. A cat showing a vestige of a tail is called a 'stumpy'.

should be a decided hollow at the end of the backbone at the point where, in the ordinary cat, the tail would begin. The hind-quarters in a Manx cannot be too high, and the back, where there must be a great depth of flank, cannot be too short. The head is round and large, but not of the snubby or Persian type. The nose is longish, but the very prominent cheeks prevent the nose appearing over-elongated, which is a bad fault. The ears are rather wide at the base, tapering slightly off to a point. Eye colour is a very secondary consideration, and must only be taken into account when all other points are equal. In such cases, the eye colour follows the ideal for the British cats, that is, blue for Whites, amber or orange for Blacks, oranges for Tortoiseshells and so on. All colours of Manx are recognized, although marking and colour, just as eye colour, must be taken into account only when all other points are equal.

Abyssinian Cats

This foreign short-hair originated in Britain. In colour and type, the Abyssinian should be ruddy brown, with black or dark brown, double or treble ticking. Two or three bands of colour on each hair are preferable to single ticking. The inside of the forelegs and belly should be of a tint which harmonizes well with the main colour, which should preferably be orange-brown.

There should be no markings such as bars on head, tail, face and chest. However, the judge must not attach such undue importance to this property that he fails to give due importance to others. For instance, it does not follow that an absolutely unmarked cat, which has a cobby build and is failing in ticking and colour, is better than a cat of slender built, well-ticked and of nice colour, but handicapped by a certain amount of 'barring' on the legs and tail.

Abyssinian and (*right*) Red Abyssinian

The Red Abyssinian is the same in every respect as the standard Abyssinian except for colour, which should be rich copper-red body colour, doubly, or preferably trebly, ticked with darker colours. Lack of distinct contrast in the ticking is considered a fault as is a pale body colour.

Standards for Abyssinian Cats

Head and ears: head long and pointed. Ears sharp, comparatively large and broad at the base.

Eyes: large, bright, and expressive, green, yellow or hazel.

Tail: fairly long and tapering.

Feet: small, black pads; this colour also extending up the back of hind-legs.

Coat: short, fine and close.

Size: never large or coarse.

Scale of points: colour – body colour 30 and ticking 20; head and ears 15; eyes 5; body shape, tail, feet, coat and carriage 20; general condition 10.

Although imperfect cats may be awarded prizes according to the merit of the entry, no Abyssinian that has distinct bars and rings on its legs and tail, should be awarded a champion certificate. A white chin should be considered undesirable, and other white markings are not permissible.

The Siamese, with its elegant proportions, is one of the most beautiful and popular cats.

Siamese Seal-pointed Cats

The Siamese is the most numerous and popular of all the foreign type breeds. Like the Russian and Abyssinian, there is no evidence whatsoever to support stories linking this cat's name with its place of origin.

Standards for Siamese Seal-pointed Cats

Shape (body and tail): medium in size, long, svelte body; proportionately slim legs; hind-legs slightly higher than the front ones; small, oval feet; long, tapering tail (either straight or slightly kinked at the extremity). The body, legs, feet, head and tail should all be in proportion, giving the whole a well-balanced appearance.

Head and ears: long, well-proportioned head, with width between the eyes, narrowing in perfectly straight lines to a fine muzzle. Ears rather large and pricked, wide at the base.

Eyes (colour and shape): clear, brilliant, deep blue. Oriental shape, slanting towards the nose. No tendency to squint.

Body colour: cream, shading gradually into pale warm fawn on the back. Kittens paler in colour.

Points: mask, ears, legs, feet and tail dense and clearly defined seal-brown. Mask complete and (except in kittens) connected by tracing with the ears.

Coat: very short and fine in texture, glossy and close lying.
Definition of squint: when the eyes are so placed that they appear to look permanently at the nose.

The Siamese Cat should be a beautifully balanced animal with head, ears and neck carried on a long, svelte body, supported on fine legs and feet, with a tail in proportion. The head and profile should be wedge-shaped, being neither round nor pointed. A green tinge in the eyes is considered a fault. The cat's expression should be alert and intelligent.

White toes – even one white toe – automatically disqualify an exhibit. It is important to note that the standard with regard to type and shape is the same for all Siamese Cats.
Scale of points for Siamese: head 15; ears 5; eyes 5; body 15; legs and paws 5; tail 5; eyes 15; points 10; body colour 10; texture of coat 10; condition 5.

Siamese Seal-pointed

Siamese Chocolate and Blue-pointed Cats

The Siamese is affectionate and delights in human company. It is unlikely to stray. It can be very demanding, with its loud, insistent voice which is quite different from that of other cats. A Siamese in season may be too loud for comfort, but in every other way it makes an attractive, lively and intelligent pet. It can be easily trained to walk on a lead.

In Britain, all colours are recognized. The Seal-pointed has already been discussed. The Chocolate-pointed is a lighter shade than the Seal-pointed. The points, that is, the ears, mask, legs, paws and tail must all be the same colour – milk chocolate. The ears should not be darker than the other points.

Standards for Siamese Chocolate-pointed Cats

Eyes: clear, bright, vivid blue.

Chocolate-pointed and (*below*) Blue-pointed Siamese.

Body: ivory colour all over. If there is any shading, it must be the colour of points.

The standard for the Blue-pointed Siamese is the same as the Chocolate-pointed with the following exceptions: the points must be blue, the ears, mask, legs, paws and tail being the same colour. The ears should not be darker than the other points.

Standards for Siamese Blue-pointed Cats

Eyes: clear, bright, vivid blue.

Body: glacial white, shading gradually into blue on back, the same cold tone as the points, but of a lighter shade.

Siamese Lilac-pointed and Red-pointed Cats

The Siamese Lilac-pointed Cat is sometimes known in the United States as the Frost-pointed. The standard is the same as for Seal-pointed, except that the eyes should be clear, bright, vivid blue. Points should be frosty grey, of pinkish tone, with nose-leather and pads faded lilac. The body-colour should be off-white (magnolia), shading, if any, to tone with points.

The Red-point Siamese is now a recognized breed in Britain. The Governing Council of the Cat Fancy in Britain describe the colour as white, with shading, if any, to apricot on the back. Ears, mask, legs, feet and tail should be bright reddish gold and the eyes, bright vivid blue. There is a modification: Barring or striping on the mask, legs or tail is not to be deemed a fault.

Lilac-pointed Siamese

French Birman Cat

French Birman Cats: Sacred Cats of Burma

This French long-hair breed was only recently recognized in Britain. According to French legend, many years before Buddha, an old priest who had a white cat lived in the mountains of Indo-China. One day when the man lay dying in front of a golden statue of a goddess with sapphire eyes, the cat jumped on to the throne. As the man died, his soul passed into the cat. The cat's fur became the golden colour of the statue, and its yellow eyes, sapphire-blue. The only unchanged parts were the tips of the paws which were touching its dead master's head. The American Cat Fanciers' Association do not give this breed official recognition.

Standards for French Birman Cats

Body: long on low legs. Short, strong paws. Front paws white, back paws white up back of foot. Even markings.
Head: wide, round, but with full cheeks.

Fur: long with good full ruff. Bushy tail, silky texture, slightly curled on belly. *Eyes:* bright china blue.
Tail: bushy (not short).
Colour and condition: the colouring is the same as Siamese, Seal and Blue, but the face, tail, and paws are dark brown with the Seals, and blue-grey with the Blues. The beige of the coat is slightly golden, the paws white gloved.
Scale of points: body 20; head 20; fur 25; eyes 5, tail 10.

Turkish Cats

Little known as yet and still unrecognized by the Governing Council of the British Cat Fancy, the Turkish Cat is making appcarances at exhibitions. This cat actually originates from Turkey and a pair of cats have been imported into Britain from Turkey which appear to breed absolutely true. This breed has a thick, white coat, with auburn head and tail, ringed in light and dark shades. The nose, ears and pads are shell-pink, and the large and lustrous eyes are amber.

Turkish Cat

Burmese Cats

Standards for Burmese Cats

Colour: in full maturity the body should be a solid, rich, dark seal-brown colour, shading to a slightly lighter colour on chest and belly white or tabby markings. Ears, mask and points only slightly darker than back coat colour. Awards should be withheld from mature cats showing a decided contrast between coat colour and points. In kittens and young cats, all colours may be slightly lighter, with greater contrast permissible between coat and points.
Shape and tail: the tail should be medium in size, dainty, long and svelte. Long, slender neck. Legs proportionately slim, hind-legs slightly higher than the front. Feet small and oval in shape. Long tail tapering to a point, a slight kink at the extreme tip only is permissible.
Head and ears: head should be a short wedge with slight rounding on top. Ears pricked, relatively large and wide at the base.
Eyes: yellow. Almond-shaped and slanting towards the nose in true oriental fashion. Blue eyes and squints inadmissible.

Blue Burmese Cat

Brown Burmese Cat

Coat: glossy, short, fine in texture, lying close to the body.
Condition: excellent physical condition, not fat, inclined to muscle.
Scale of points: shape and tail 25; head and ears 15; eyes 15; coat 10; condition 10.

Blue Burmese Cats

Colour is the only difference between the two Burmese Cats. The body colour of the adult Blue Burmese should be predominantly bluish-grey, darker on the back, the overall effect being a warm colour, with a silver sheen on the coat. The tail colour should be the same as the back, with no white or tabby markings.

The American Cat Fanciers' Association describe the Burmese as being midway between domestic short-hairs and Siamese in body structure. It does not list the Blue Burmese as a recognized breed.

Chestnut-brown or Havana Cats

This cat was once known in Britain as the Havana but the name was dropped to avoid legends springing up about its origin although in the United States, the breed is still known as the Havana. It is a product of the British breeders and arose, in the first instance, from a mismating of a Black Long-hair female with a Seal-pointed Siamese. One of the black female kittens born as a result was again mated with Siamese and one of the litter carried the chocolate gene of the Siamese. It was a Self-brown male. The difference between it and the Burmese lies in the shape of its body. The Burmese is broader and more compact, while the Chestnut-brown more closely resembles the Russian Blue in type. The Burmese also has a distinctly darker colour at the points, whereas the Chestnut-brown is a rich, warm, mahogany-brown all over, altogether a warmer colour.

The Governing Council of the Cat Fancy in Britain state that the eyes should be slanting and oriental in shape. In the United States, the Cat Fanciers' Association state that the chartreuse-green eyes should be oval in shape and set almost straight.

The head should be set on a graceful but not a long neck. The head should also be longer than its width, with ears set wider apart than the Siamese, and pricked forward. The Americans say it has a *pixie look*.

Chestnut-brown Cats are of the foreign type. They are fine in bone, lithe, sinuous, and of graceful proportions. The coat is rich brown, even and sound. Whiskers and nose should be of the same colour as the coat. The pads of the feet are a pinkish shade. The eyes are green.

Standards for Chestnut-brown Cats

Coat: any shade of rich chestnut-brown, short and glossy, even and sound throughout.

Head and ears: long, well-proportioned head, narrowing to a fine muzzle. Large, pricked ears, wide at the base with good width between.

Body, legs and tail: body long, lithe and well-muscled, graceful in outline. Slim, dainty legs, hind-legs slightly higher than front legs. Paws oval and neat. Long whip tail, no kink.

Eyes: slanting and oriental in shape, decidedly green in colour.
Scale of points: coat 30; head 15; body 15; legs 15; tail 5; eyes 10; condition 10.
Faults: tabby or other markings, dark points, white spots or hairs, cobby shape, round head, short, thick or kinked tail.

Kittens frequently show tabby 'ghost' markings when changing coat. This should not be held against an otherwise good kitten.

The Chestnut-brown Cat

Rex Cats

Breeds of cats have, until recently, been divided into two types, the long-hair and the short-hair. In all these cats, the hair is straight. One of the newest introductions to breeds of cats, however, is called *rex-coated*. Each individual hair of this coat is waved and no guard hairs are visible, because they are shortened to just below the level of the top coat. The hair is considerably shorter than that of other short-haired types, giving an extremely soft, short coat with tiny marcel-like waves.

Geneticists believe that the rex came about as a mutation involving a single recessive factor. For this reason, the hair type can be transferred to any breed, colour or type of cat. As a result, the variety of cat to which this factor is transfered will retain all its characteristics, except that its coat will become rex type.

In Great Britain, the Governing Council of the Cat Fancy now recognize two breeds of rex-coated cats. They are the Cornish Rex-coated Cat Gene 1 and the Devon Rex-coated Cat Gene 2.

In the United States, the Cat Fanciers' Association have recognized the Rex Cat as a breed and set the following standards:

Head: should be longer than it is wide, with a break at the muzzle when viewed from the front, and with a Roman profile.

Eyes: should be medium-size, oval in shape. Colour in keeping with the coat colour.

Tail: long and slender, tapering slightly. No penalty for a bare upper surface.

Body: long and slender, with a *tuck-up* behind the ribs. Hips heavy in proportion to the rest of the body. Body hard and muscular.

American standard of points

Head: shape, muzzle break 5; profile 3; chin 2; total for head 10; neck should be medium long and slender 5; ears, large and naked, set high on head 5; eyes 5; tail 5; body 10; tuck-up 5; legs 5; texture 10; density 10; waviness 10; colour and markings (as for Manx Cat) 10; condition 5; balance 5. Disqualification occurs for coarse or guard hairs.

Mexican Hairless, and Peke-faced Persian Cats

The Mexican Hairless is thought to be almost extinct. Like the dog of the same name, the Mexican Hairless does in fact have some very short, close hair. The neck and underparts are pinkish, and the back is mouse-coloured. The cat is adapted to high temperatures and, in winter, it develops a ridge of fur along the back and upper surface of its tail.

A cat recognized in the United States, but not in Britain, is the Peke-faced Persian. This breed has developed because of the heavy jowls shown by some of the Long-haired Reds and Red Tabby Cats. The head on this cat resembles that of the Pekinese dog. Not only must the forehead be high, but it must also bulge over the nose to create a sharp *stop*. The nose must be short, depressed, and indented between the eyes. In profile, the nose should be concealed by the full, round cheeks. The muzzle should be decidedly wrinkled with folds of skin from each side of the nose and under the eye sockets. The eyes must be very round, large and full. The coat colour may be Red Tabby or Red Self.

Himalayan Cats

The Himalayan Cat of the United States is basically the same as the British Colourpoint. It is a Persian Cat to which the Siamese colour pattern has been transferred. The standard for the breed is the same as for the Persian. Whereas the Colourpoint is recognized in only three of the Siamese colourings, the Himalayan has breed numbers for five. They are the Blue-point, Red-point, Frost-point, Seal-point, and Chocolate-point.

Peke-faced Persian Cat

Himalayan Cat

Mexican Hairless Cats

Maine Coon Cat, Odd-eyed White and (*below*) Shell Cameo

Shell Cameos

The Shell Cameo is recognized as an American long-haired breed. It is not, however, recognized by the Governing Council in Britain.

This cat must conform to the general standards of the regular Persian and the pattern is the same as that for the Silvers. There are three shades and patterns in the Cameos.

The Shell Cameo has hairs on the back, flanks, head and tail that must be sufficiently tipped with red to give a tinsel effect. The ground colour is ivory-white. As in the Silvers and the Chinchillas, the colour must produce a sparkling effect. The face and legs are lightly shaded with tipping, but the ear tufts, belly, chest and undersides of the tail must be untipped. No tabby markings or fawn tinge are allowed. Eyes are copper. Eye rims and nose leather are brick-pink.

The Shaded Cameo has red tipping that is considerably heavier than that on the Shell. This gives the cat a *hot* glow, but the colour diminishes gradually into the sides to meet the ivory-white of the undersides.

The Smoke Cameo has the same colour pattern as the Black- and Blue-Smokes. The rich, red tipping rests on a creamy-white ground colour. In short, the coat looks like that of a solid Red until the coat is parted. No tabby markings or brown tinge are permitted.

Maine Coon and Odd-eyed White Cats

The Maine Coon Cat is an American breed, which has no show standing, but is a variant domestic. New Englanders once thought that it was a cross between cat and raccoon, which explains the origin of its name. Nowadays experts believe it to be full-blooded Angora.

Frequently the forelegs of this cat present a slight toeing-in effect similar to those of a raccoon. The head is pointed and the eyes, though perfectly round, often show a slight slant. The tail is the reverse of that of the Persian, with the longest hairs being at the base.

The Odd-eyed White is a recognized breed in the United States. The standard calls for one blue and one deep orange eye. The coat should be short and thick, even in texture, and pure white in colour.

SHOWING CATS

Pedigree cats arouse public interest throughout the world. Cat clubs and societies organize shows in many countries. In Britain, the Governing Council of the Cat Fancy agrees the standards and the scale of points for the various breeds. It also grants challenge certificates to winning cats at championship shows.

To become a full champion, a cat must win three challenge certificates at three separate shows under three different judges. The highest award a cat can achieve is that of an International Champion. To gain this award, it must become the champion in another country after having first attained the award in its own country.

Preparation

To prepare your cat for showing, the first aim is to see that it is in perfect coat. You can do a great deal to improve its appearance. A light-coloured cat will benefit from a little dry cleaning a few days before the show. Fuller's earth, bran, or one of the proprietary cat-cleaning powders are all suitable. Particular attention should be given to the tail of the white cat, because grease tends to make it yellow. A cat with a yellow, greasy tail would be placed down at the show. It is advisable not to powder on the morning of the show. If any powder were left in the coat, this would lead to disqualification. All dirt and grease must be removed, and the eyes must be perfectly clean.

Long-haired cats will need extra special attention on the morning of the show. Intensive grooming will have started a month beforehand, but a last brush and comb with special attention to the ruff should be given.

Short-haired cats will benefit from a final rub over with a piece of velvet or chamois leather. This method produces a beautiful sheen. To sum up, your cat must be in perfect health and groomed to perfection.

Judges handle cats carefully but firmly and examine them closely to discover all their good and bad points.

Arrival at the show

A veterinary surgeon examines all cats before the show, looking into the cat's fur, eyes, ears and throat to check for signs of parasites, skin disease or any other infection. If there is any doubt about their state of health, the cats will be refused entry. The schedule for the show will have been received when the owner sends in the entry form. The schedule should be read with care, because it lists the various classes, entry fees and awards. It also gives the regulations for the day of the show.

The cat must be taken to the show by the owner, or by a personal representative. The cat will be allocated a pen bearing the same number as the disc which the cat should be wearing on a ribbon around its neck and it is advisable that a cat is accustomed to a show pen before attempts are made to exhibit it.

It is a good idea to visit some cat shows, to study the cats that win prizes and compare them with one's own cat, and thus see what is required.

Judging

During the judging, all exhibitors must leave the hall. Unlike the procedure at dog shows exhibitors of cats are not allowed to handle their pets while judging is in progress. Stewards carry the cats from their pens to the judges for their inspection. Judges have expert knowledge of cats and are scrupulously fair. In addition to challenge certificates, rosettes and cups, the first, second and third in the various classes receive prize money. This is paid later, when all entries have been checkcd by the Governing Council of the Cat Fancy.

At cat shows, all cats are handled with carc and understanding and most cats soon adapt to show conditions. Somc cats, liowever, are too nervous even when handled patiently and should not in this case be shown. However beautiful a specimen is it will not show to advantage if it is always frightened of strangers and strange surroundings.

During the show

Pens at shows are always provided and owners are not allowed to use their own. However, great care is taken and they are always perfectly clean. As a further precaution, it is as well to wipe the bars and backing lightly with methylated spirit or some mild disinfectant. Nothing is allowed into the pen but a piece of white blanket which is folded flat, and a sanitary tin. Peat moss for the sanitary tins will be found in the hall.

The cat should not be given any food within two hours of going to the show, nor should it be fed during the show until the judging is over. It should be remembered that milk is a food and not a drink. A little clean drinking water is permitted in the pens and drinking bowls are provided, although owners may prefer to take their own.

Most shows are over by 6 p.m. If an exhibitor lives more than a hundred miles away and wishes to leave a little earlier, however, permission to leave can be applied for when the entry form is sent in.

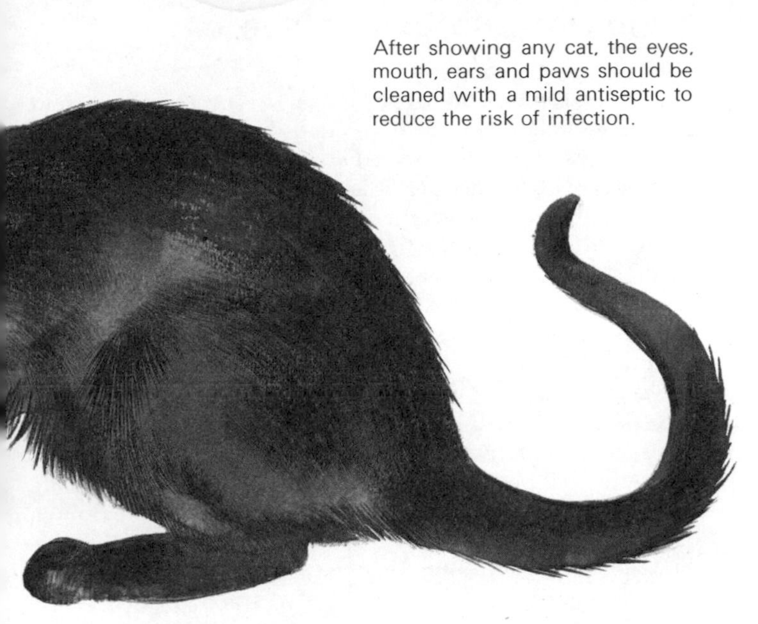
After showing any cat, the eyes, mouth, ears and paws should be cleaned with a mild antiseptic to reduce the risk of infection.

After the show

Even though care is taken, there is always risk of infection when a number of cats are gathered together. Some exhibitors like to put a sheet of clear plastic over the front of the pen and so prevent people touching their cat through the bars. This can prevent the innocent passing on of infection from one pen to the next.

After the show the eyes, mouth, ears and paws should be cleaned with a mild disinfectant to reduce the risk. The cat should be taken home as quickly as possible and given a good meal. A few drops of brandy in milk will help to revive its spirits and keep away chills if the weather is cold. Its bed should be placed away from draughts, because show halls tend to become overheated and cats are susceptible to colds. If there are other cats in the house, the exhibited cat should be kept away from the others for at least a week and the owner should wash and change before coming in contact with them, as yet another precaution against the passing on of dangerous infections.

Serious cat diseases

Cats are particularly hardy animals, especially the short-haired varieties, but there are two diseases to be dreaded. The first is *Feline Infectious Enteritis,* the most devastating of all cat diseases, because it is fatal in about eighty per cent of cases. Immediate veterinary treatment should be sought if a cat loses its appetite, appears to be thirsty but is unable to drink, is sick and has a temperature. Kittens should be immunized soon after leaving their mother. If a cat dies from this disease, all the cat's bedding must be burnt and the house disinfected.

Vaccination for Feline Infectious Enteritis gives a small measure of protection from the second killer disease, which is *Feline Distemper* or cat 'flu. The symptoms are coughing, sneezing, and nasal and eye discharge. The cat loses weight, and, although the illness is a long one, the cat may be brought back to good health with careful nursing. There is as yet no vaccine specifically for this disease and, as with all serious ailments, expert veterinary attention is essential.

If a cat loses its appetite, it should receive veterinary attention immediately.

Other cat ailments

A cat involved in a fight with a rat or another cat may receive a bite which can cause an *abscess*. A swelling develops which has a shiny appearance and is painful to the touch. Veterinary assistance is needed but meanwhile bathing in hot water will help to bring the abscess to a head.

Canker should never be neglected. The cat will be seen frequently shaking its head, scratching its ears and rubbing its head against hard surfaces. There are a number of good lotions for the condition and treatment should be repeated daily until the ear is clean. A weekly inspection and powdering with one of the proprietary powders should prevent further trouble.

A cat with *fleas* is constantly scratching. These must be removed, because fleas are carriers of disease and can spread tapeworm. Powders which contain DDT should never be used. Pyrethrum is the most up-to-date of all flea remedies and is absolutely harmless to the cat. Both the cat and its sleeping quarters should be treated because fleas' eggs drop off the body of the host and can lie dormant for months until conditions are right for them to hatch.

If a cat is scratching frequently, it may have canker, fleas, ear discharge or some other kind of irritation, and should be checked closely.

How to obtain a kitten

If one wants a kitten, but is not particular as to the sort of cat one has, then the best thing to do is answer one of the innumerable advertisements in local newspapers. There are always kittens going 'free to a good home' and, although the cat that is adopted from the local welfare society, or the stray that just appears on the doorstep, may appear unattractive at first appearance, many of them grow into fine-looking cats with care and attention. Care should be taken to see that a 'stray' really does not have an owner. Some cats will visit anyone who will feed them regularly.

Kittens can also be obtained from pet shops for a fee that depends really on the parentage of the cat. If a pedigree cat of a particular breed is wanted, then it will be necessary to pay much more for it. When the breed has been decided on, the secretary of that breed's society will supply the addresses of breeders in the neighbourhood. It is much better to obtain a kitten when it is young because then it can be trained to fit in with the routine of the household. One that is less than six weeks old, however, should never be bought. It is not old enough to leave its mother.

Choosing a kitten

It is possible to form a rough idea of the age of a kitten by examining its mouth. Never buy a kitten that has not got a full set of small, sharp, white teeth in each jaw. The inside of the mouth should be a clear, rosy-pink. If the milk teeth are only just beginning to show, the kitten is not properly weaned and will be naturally weak. It is practically certain to have digestive troubles.

Female kittens are usually less expensive than males, and the possibility that she could be the mother of numerous families should not deter anyone who is looking for a pet. Although the operation to make a female neuter is slightly more difficult than that for a male, it can successfully be done from an age of four months onwards, providing it is done by a skilled veterinarian. The process is called spaying, and spayed females are gentle and affectionate pets.

Plenty of time must be allowed when choosing a kitten, because cats are creatures of great individuality and you are going to spend many years in each other's company. Look at the whole litter, for there will be one that is quite definitely the leader. If one wants an affectionate companion, the leader should be avoided. On the other hand, if one of the kittens is not inclined to play, this one should also be avoided. A nervous kitten will bush its tail and back away from people. Pull a piece of string and shake it about. Notice which kitten is most eager to play and is quickest in its reactions. It will soon be possible to decide which kitten has the most appeal from its behaviour.

Assessing a kitten's health

The kitten in the litter which appeals most should be examined closely. Its eyes should be clear and bright. If any kitten in the litter has runny eyes, do not buy a kitten from that litter. Next look at the ears. Do not touch them, but make sure they are clean and do not smell and never buy a kitten with dirty or smelly ears. If one is gentle with the kitten, stroking and talking to it, it will be ready to snuggle close and it will be possible to run a hand lightly over its body. There should be no roughness anywhere and if any roughness can be felt, part the hairs to make sure that it is not a sore. It may only be a scratch from play, but if it is a sore, it would be advisable to leave the whole litter alone.

The stomach of a healthy kitten should feel firm and rubbery. A hard or flabby tummy is a bad sign, but a choice can safely be made from others in the litter. A swollen stomach may indicate rickets or worms and although it is possible to clear this trouble up with medication it is better not to start with this problem.

Introducing the kitten to its new home

Unless the prospective owner lives within walking distance of the breeder, a basket will be necessary to carry the kitten home. Arriving at its new home is a strange and possibly terrifying experience for a kitten. Until this moment, it has had a mother to protect it and brothers and sisters to play with and snuggle against for warmth. The first few days are a time for adjustment, when the kitten needs all the love and attention you can give it. It is best to introduce the kitten into its new home when one has plenty of time to spend with it. It should be allowed to explore its surroundings and be accompanied while it explores, because it should also get to know its owner. Talk to it quietly for conversation is important, and the kitten will soon understand the different tones of voice and this will be a help throughout its life. At first, a warm hot-water bottle at night will take the place of its brothers and sisters. It will need a lot of petting, but never attempt to hold it against its will. And remember that it requires plenty of sleep.

Training

Cats are naturally clean animals. The mother teaches its kittens to conceal the evidence of their presence and so there is usually no difficulty with house-training. All that is needed is a flat tray, such as a baking tray, and something it can dig into, such as sand, ashes or soil. Place the kitten in the tray and, holding its front paws, go through the scratching motions. It will soon realize what is required of it. Should a kitten misbehave never, never 'rub its nose in it' because punishment is not the slightest use. Take the kitten to its tray and go through the scratching movements again. Clean the soiled spot thoroughly and put down a repellent, so that the kitten will not use the place again. A cat will not use a dirty tray. The contents should be changed regularly and the tray itself should be washed frequently to keep it free from odour.

It is a good idea to start a kitten off with a bed of its own, although sooner or later it is bound to find a sleeping place of its own choosing. Cats like to sleep on newspaper, because it is warm and newspaper has the advantage of being easily replaced. A cushion does not make good bedding because it is difficult to wash.

A cat should be able to learn to use a dirt tray with a minimum of training.

Grooming

All domestic cats should be groomed thoroughly every day. A long-haired cat needs frequent attention and should be groomed twice every day, morning and evening. If one is unable to spare this amount of time, a short-hair should be chosen. Without regular grooming, not only will the appearance of the long-haired cat suffer but its health will also be affected.

For grooming, the cat should be stood on a table. Running a hand over its body will enable one to feel for any burs, which should be carefully removed before combing. Begin with a wide-toothed comb, using it firmly and follow with a finer comb, to get through to the under fur, removing any parasites. After combing, most cats enjoy a vigorous brushing, although many cats dislike being stroked gently with a brush. Give the first brushing from tail to head against the lie of the coat, removing loose hairs, then brush the hair down with long sweeping strokes. A rub with a chamois leather will leave the cat smart and glossy. This procedure will take longer for a long-haired cat.

Cats should have their own dishes, baskets and brushes. All cats should be groomed daily and long-hairs twice daily.

Cleaning

After grooming, the eyes, ears and feet should be examined. In this way any parasitic infection will be found before it can take hold. A dirty ear flap can be cleaned with damp cotton-wool. If wax accumulates, it should be cleaned away gently with a small piece of cotton-wool on an orange stick. Dust and dirt sometimes collect in the corners of the eyes and should also be removed with damp cotton-wool.

A split or torn claw, particularly on the hind-feet, can injure the cat when it scratches itself. A veterinary surgeon should deal with these and one must not trim the claw oneself.

Cats do not normally need baths. A cat can be cleaned very well with a moist sponge, followed by a rub down with a dry towel. A dry shampoo can also be used, but this must not be rubbed in more than one can help because it can clog the pores and set up an irritation. The dry shampoo must be brushed out thoroughly and a shampoo made especially for cats must be used. Fuller's earth may also be used for this purpose.

Feeding

Until it is three months old, a kitten's stomach is no bigger than a walnut. It cannot eat much food at one meal but it does require a lot of small meals, because it is growing very fast. The meals must be well-spaced and regular. Kittens should start the day with a milk meal; around eleven they need a meat meal, preferably beef finely chopped; lunch can be egg and milk; tea should be meat again, supper the same as lunch and meat again at bedtime. The number of meals should be reduced as the kitten grows older, until at six or seven months the milk teeth are replaced by the permanent teeth. The fully-grown cat requires only one meal a day, and milk or water to drink. A supply of fresh water should always be available whenever the cat wants it.

Fish should always be cooked. All bones, especially the little ones, should be removed before the fish is given to the cat. Working cats need more than milk if they are to give of their best. A cat or kitten that catches mice still requires feeding and cats that are fed regularly will hunt for sport. They will have the vitality and stamina to do the job.

Moving house

If one has been an understanding owner and a companionable relationship exists between oneself and one's cat, no problems should arise when the time comes to move the cat to a new home. Once the cat has been given time to settle down in its new quarters, it will not wander away and get lost. It seldom objects to a new home as long as its friends are there. It should be allowed to explore the house, feeling and smelling everything until it is satisfied that all is as it should be. The cat will then sit down and wash itself, a signal that it is ready to be fed. An old country method was to butter the cat's paws or to smear sardine oil on its chest, legs and paws. This is not such a ridiculous idea as it sounds as cleaning it off will keep the cat occupied for some time and it will be far too busy to be nervous.

If the worst happens and, despite all precautions, the cat still disappears it is best to get in touch with the neighbours at one's old address. Many cats have travelled considerable distances to return to their old homes. At least until a cat is settled in its new home it should wear an elastic collar with its new address.

Going on holiday

Before going on holiday, arrangements must be made for one's cat. Leaving it in a shed with food is not sufficient, because it would eat it all at once and go hungry for the remainder of the period. Friends, or neighbours, can sometimes be prevailed upon to feed it and shut it up at night, or it can be sent to recommended boarding kennels.

Sometimes a satisfactory solution is to take the cat with one on holiday and practically all Siamese cats make good travellers. Generally speaking, however, few cats make willing travelling companions and will, if possible, prefer to be left in their own surroundings.

If kittens are trained young enough, it may be possible to train them to walk on a lead, like a dog.

Cat travelling hamper

Moving cats

If it is essential to move a cat for a long distance it is important for the cat to have its own travelling hamper. This should be high and wide enough to allow the pet freedom of movement but not so large that the animal rolls about with the motion of a vehicle. If the case fastens with a bolt, a padlock should be put on it as well as cats can be very clever at sliding back catches. The case can be opened occasionally to pet the cat, and of course, it will hear voices if it is spoken to. The basket should be lined with newspaper and a warm blanket and if the sides are lined with paper it will protect the cat from draughts.

Some breeds, particularly Siamese, take quite naturally to the lead, and this is an advantage on a long journey because the cat can be exercised at intervals without danger of losing it. If a kitten will accept a collar, training to the lead should not be difficult, but it should begin at an early age. No grown cat will accept a collar without a struggle, if it has not been trained. Of course, providing there is no danger of escape, there is no reason why the cat cannot spend some of the time on the owner's lap.

Since cats rarely enjoy travelling it is often a good idea to ask one's vet for a tranquillizer for the cat. This can be given just before setting out and should ensure a trouble-free journey.

For short journeys, such as a visit to the veterinary surgeon, a hold-all may be used to carry the cat. The zip-fastener should be closed leaving just the cat's head free. This enables the cat to see what is going on around it and this fact alone is often sufficient to prevent the animal from becoming frightened. Care must be taken, however, to see that the cat cannot wriggle free for it is certain to be nervous and would almost certainly bolt if given a chance.

Over short distances hampers are unnecessary and a zip-fastened hold-all can be used.

Equipment

All cats must scratch regularly to keep their claws in perfect condition and frequently armchairs or table legs suffer as a result of this need to pull off the outer shells of the claws as they become worn. The action also keeps in good condition the muscles and tendons, which control the function of the claws. One can, however, protect furniture by providing a scratching post for the cat. An ordinary log, complete with bark, will serve the purpose, but it will soon become smooth and shiny and need to be replaced. A solid board upholstered with a piece of carpet is preferable. The kitten must be taught at an early stage that the board is for its use, in a manner very similar to that used when teaching it to use its sand tray. Hold its paw and put it through the motions of scratching on the post.

Grass is a natural medicine for cats and its action as an emetic is often the means of inducing the vomiting of a hair-ball, which forms in the cat's stomach, especially during the moulting season. For cats living in a flat, grass can be grown in pots or boxes, Cocks-foot grass seems to be particularly favoured. To ensure a regular supply of grass for a cat, a fresh pot or box should be sown every week or ten days.

As has been mentioned previously, kittens can be taught to wear a collar and leash and special ones made for cats can be obtained at most pet shops.

Old logs make good scratching posts.

Toys for cats should be hygenic and not contain any loose or dangerous parts.

Toys

Play is a necessary part of a kitten's exercise and it will invent the most exciting games with simple things like fallen leaves or a screwed-up piece of paper. An empty packet tied on a length of string and left to dangle within reach will give your cat hours of pleasure. Cats also like playing with a ping-pong ball or an empty cotton reel. Most cats appreciate a rubber mouse. Your cat will probably enjoy a toy mouse, with or without catmint filling. Since catmint is a herb which is the delight of adult cats, these mice will soon become a tasty snack. Toys should not have any sharp parts which the cat could swallow. Rubber balls are fun too but they must be too big to swallow.

Putting the cat out

In the past, people put the cat out at night along with the milk bottles. Today cat owners are more intelligent, and they realize they have a responsibility to their pets. It is unkind to send a cat deliberately out of doors at night, especially in bad weather. This custom has made many enemies for the cat. It is true that cats are nocturnal animals and are not deterred by darkness. But their worst offence is destroying birds. Fewer birds would be eaten if cats were trained to come into the house at dusk. Cats like to hunt and they are most likely to attack at dawn when the birds are feeding.

A cat left to roam at night is also more likely to annoy neighbours with caterwauling. In built-up areas, there is danger from speeding vehicles. In fact, a cat allowed to stay home at night is less likely to come to grief than one that is left to its own devices. Staying in at night should be a matter of training and not compulsion. Cats enjoy their freedom and should be given ready access to the garden whenever they feel a need to go out.

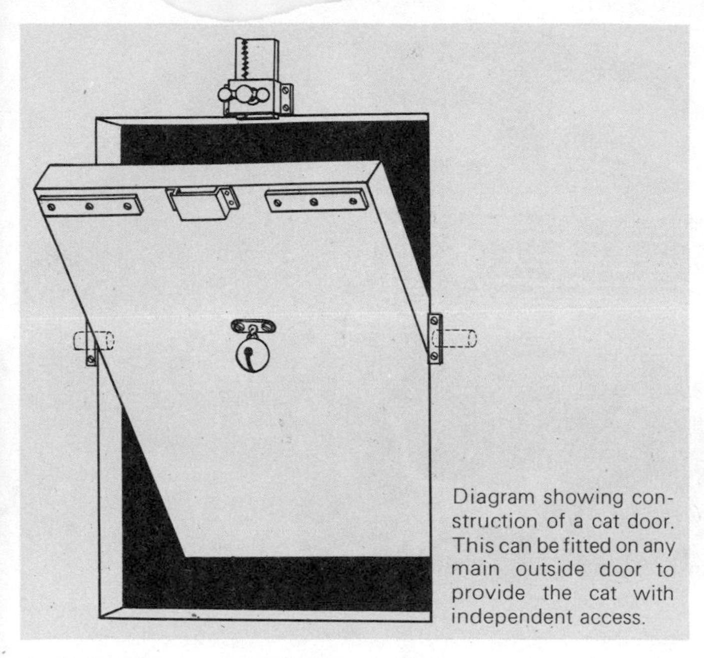

Diagram showing construction of a cat door. This can be fitted on any main outside door to provide the cat with independent access.

Cat door

The simplest way to ensure complete freedom for the cat, so that it may come and go as it wishes, is to have a cat door fitted to one of the outside doors of the house. The cat will soon learn to use the door and will greatly value this recognition of his independence.

The opening for the door need not be large, because cats can squeeze through quite a small hole. It can be about 6 inches by 4 inches and should swing vertically on a hinge so that it can be opened from either side. It is important to see that the cat door is fitted with weights so that it closes slowly, giving time for the cat's tail to clear the door. The door should be so positioned, however, that it is out of reach of bolts or locks as a prevention against burglaries. If more owners took the initial trouble to have a cat door fitted they would find it considerably more convenient than having to provide and keep changing a sand tray somewhere in the house.

THE LAW AND THE PROTECTION OF CATS

Britain has no statutory laws dealing with cats. Cats are classed as wild animals. They are untaxed and are treated as uncontrolled animals. For this reason, the owner of a cat cannot be held responsible for its actions. This does not mean the cat has no legal rights. It is a domestic animal according to the law and in Britain is protected by the Animal Protection Act (1911), the Cruelty to Animals Act and the Abandonment of Animals Act. Because the cat is classified as a wild animal it is untaxed, and of no interest to the State, and unlike the dog, cats are not covered by the Road Traffic Act. It is not necessary, therefore, to report an accident involving a cat.

At Common Law, cats formerly fell within the exception to the rule that domestic and tame animals were larcenable. Now, however, the owners of cats are protected by statute.

Similar legislation to protect the cat exists in countries of the British Commonwealth, and the United States is very strict on animal care. Some places, such as Saddle Brook, New Jersey, have laws that insist cats are belled and licensed.

No British cat owner can be held legally responsible for the misdeeds of his pet. He cannot, for example, be held responsible if his cat kills the neighbour's birds, or damages his plants, but he should prevent the animal becoming a nuisance to his neighbours. Loving care and good training will teach the cat all that is required, but since a domestic cat is not normally confined, there may be occasions when the ncighbour's garden suffers.

In Britain, the law states that anyone who ill-treats, beats, kicks, frightens, or commits any action that will cause

unnecessary suffering to a cat is liable to a fine or to imprisonment. Any person who through cruelty causes damage or injury to a cat is liable to pay compensation to its owner. The law also states that:

Any cat owner who fails to protect his cat from cruelty or by failing to do any act causes unnecessary suffering to the animal, is liable to a fine or to imprisonment or both.

Anyone who knowingly puts down poison for vermin without taking precautions to prevent injury to any cat, is liable to a fine.

A person who performs any operation on a cat without due care and humanity, causes anyone to do this, or allows his cat to be operated upon in this manner, is liable to a fine or imprisonment or to both.

Anyone who performs the operation of castration upon a kitten without anaesthetic, or, being a cat owner, allows this to be done to his cat is liable to a fine or imprisonment or both.

In addition to the hazards of everyday life a cat has to face the danger of being hunted by cat haters or cat collectors. In New York there is a state conservation law relating to cats, that decrees that:

Any person over the age of twenty-one years possessing a hunting licence may, and game protectors and other peace officers, shall, humanely destroy cats at large found hunting or killing any bird protected by law, or with a dead bird of any species protected by law in its possession, and no action for damages shall lie for such killing.

The Royal Society for the Prevention of Cruelty to Animals in Britain, similar societies in the British Commonwealth, and the American Humane Association in the United States, deal with many cases every year concerned with cruelty to cats. Neglect or cruelty should be reported to the local officers or to the headquarters of such societies.

Quarantine

To prevent the introduction of rabies into Britain, imported cats are subject to detention, at the owners' expense, in an approved place of quarantine. The United States has no restrictions but requires a health certificate showing that the cat is free from infectious disease and has not been in contact with an animal infected with rabies. Australia has very strict quarantine regulations.

Strays

If some owners of domestic pets had more moral sense, the problem of unwanted cats would be far less. People going on holiday, who leave a cat to fend for itself, cannot expect it to know that they will return in a short time. Sometimes people abandon a cat once it is past the playful stage, turning it out in favour of another, more playful, kitten.

A little more care would prevent these cats joining the vast population of strays. Should a stray turn up on your doorstep and decide to adopt you, it would be as well to have it examined by a veterinary surgeon before taking it in, particularly if you have other cats. The life of a stray is hard and it is prey to diseases of all kinds. Until suitable arrangements can be made, the cat should be given a good meal outside the house.

There are several societies which help the cat that has no home and no one to care for it.

Cat protection societies

Many humane societies all over the world devote themselves to the welfare of animals. In Britain, the Cat's Protection League is the only society devoting itself entirely to the welfare of cats and kittens. The work of the league is to alleviate suffering, to find homes for unwanted kittens, to provide medical attention and to advise on care and feeding. The league does a great deal of educational work and a number of leaflets are published by the league dealing with various aspects of cat protection and welfare. Similar work is undertaken in America by the American Feline Society.

The address of the General Secretary of the Cat's Protection League is 29 Church Street, Slough, Buckinghamshire. The

National Headquarters of the American Feline Society Inc. is 41 Union Square West, New York, N.Y. 10003.

Other animal societies are concerned with the care of animals in general, including the American Humane Association in the United States. The Royal Society for the Prevention of Cruelty to Animals in Britain is the oldest animal protection society in the world. Several societies in the British Commonwealth are affiliated to the RSPCA. The RSPCA investigates cases of ill-treatment and cruelty, and sees that the laws concerning animals are carried out. The People's Dispensary for Sick Animals and the Blue Cross Society advise on all matters concerning the cat's health and provide free treatment for those that cannot afford the fees.

All these charitable organizations rely entirely upon subscriptions, legacies and donations.

The Feline Advisory Bureau

The Feline Advisory Bureau in Britain is a national organization which was founded in 1958. It has two main objects. Generally its aim is to promote humane behaviour towards the cat and to assure its physical well-being by giving advice to its owner on its maintenance in health, and care in sickness. A great deal of research is carried out by the bureau into feline disorders and a central fund has been established for feline research. Sufficient funds will enable the bureau to sponsor investigations into the various cat diseases which are not yet fully understood and for which no effective treatment exists.

The advisory service is based on an up-to-date survey of appropriate literature and reference to recognized authorities. An extensive reference library is maintained and there is also a panel of scientific, medical and veterinary experts. Contributions to the Central Fund for Feline Research will speed investigations into cat diseases. Application for membership should be made to the Honorary Secretary, Mrs Joan Judd, The Barn Cottage, Tytherington, Wotton-Under-Edge, Gloucestershire. Members receive details of scientific data added to the library and copies of the papers listed are available on loan upon application to Mrs R. Goodwin, 92 Church Road, Horley, Surrey.

BOOKS TO READ

A Practical Cat Book by I. M. Mellen. Scribner, New York, 1939.

Atlas of Anatomy by H. E. Field and M. E. Taylor. University of Chicago Press, 1964.

Book of the Cat by Francis Simpson. Cassell, London, 1903.

Caring for your Cat by W. Thatcher and A. W. Richards. Foyles, London, 1966.

Cat Musculature by G. M. Greenblatt. University of Chicago Press, 1954.

Cats and their Care by Rose Tenant. Arthur Barker Ltd, London, 1965.

Diseases of the Cat by G. Thompson Wilkinson. Pergamon Press, Oxford, 1966.

History of Domestic Animals by F. E. Zeuner. British Museum Natural History, London, 1963

How to Look After your Pet by M. Hamilton-Wilkes, Angus and Robertson, Sydney, 1967.

Looking after your Cat by J. Montgomery. Allen and Unwin, London, 1964.

Observers Book of Cats by Grace Pond. Frederick Warne, London, 1968.

Pedigree Cats, their Varieties, Breeding and Exhibition by P. M. Soderberg. Cassell, London, 1958.

Science and Mystery of the Cat by I. M. Mellen. Scribner, New York, 1940.

The Basic Book of the Cat by William H. A. Carr. Stanley Paul, London, 1965.

The Cat by St George Mivart. John Murray, London, 1881.

The Cat: Facts about Fantasy by N. R. Haworth. Heineman Medical Books, London, 1966.

The Cat in Mysteries of Religion and Magic by Oldfield Howey. Rider, London, 1930.

The Cat Owners Encyclopaedia by Brian Vesey-Fitzgerald. Pelham, London, 1963.

The Cat Owners Guide by John P. Volrath. Universities Federation for Animal Welfare, London, 1960.

The Encyclopedia of Witchcraft and Demonology by Russel Hope Robbins. Crown, New York, 1959.

Your Cat by P. M. Soderberg. Cassell, London, 1951

INDEX

Page numbers in bold type refer to illustrations.

SOME OTHER TITLES IN THIS SERIES

- Arts
- Domestic Animals and Pets
- Domestic Science
- Gardening
- General Information
- History and Mythology
- Natural History
- Popular Science

Arts
Antique Furniture/Architecture/Clocks and Watches/Glass for Collectors/Jewellery/Musical Instruments/Porcelain/Victoriana

Domestic Animals and Pets
Budgerigars/Cats/Dog Care/Dogs/Horses and Ponies/Pet Birds/Pets for Children/Tropical Freshwater Aquaria/Tropical Marine Aquaria

Domestic Science
Flower Arranging

Gardening
Chrysanthemums/Garden Flowers/Garden Shrubs/House Plants/Plants for Small Gardens/Roses

General Information
Aircraft/Arms and Armour/Coins and Medals/Flags/Guns/Military Uniforms/National Costumes of the world/Rockets and Missiles/Sailing/Sailing Ships and Sailing Craft/Sea Fishing/Trains/Veteran and Vintage Cars/Warships

History and Mythology
Age of Shakespeare/Archaeology/Discovery of: Africa/The American West/Australia/Japan/North America/South America/Myths and Legends of: Africa/Ancient Egypt/Ancient Greece/Ancient Rome/India/The South Seas/Witchcraft and Black Magic

Natural History
The Animal Kingdom/Animals of Australia and New Zealand/Animals of Southern Asia/Bird Behaviour/Birds of Prey/Butterflies/Evolution of Life/Fishes of the world/Fossil Man/A Guide to the Seashore/ Life in the Sea/Mammals of the world/Monkeys and Apes/Natural History Collecting/The Plant Kingdom/Prehistoric Animals/Seabirds/Seashells/Snakes of the world/Trees of the World/Tropical Birds/Wild Cats

Popular Science
Astronomy/Atomic Energy/Chemistry/Computers at Work/The Earth/Electricity/Electronics/Exploring the Planets/The Human Body/Mathematics/Microscopes and Microscopic Life/Undersea Exploration/The Weather Guide